THE COMPLETE GUIDE TO
GROWING
Healing and Medicinal Herbs

Everything You Need to Know
EXPLAINED SIMPLY

REVISED 2ND EDITION

By Wendy M. Vincent

THE COMPLETE GUIDE TO GROWING HEALING AND MEDICINAL HERBS: EVERYTHING YOU NEED TO KNOW EXPLAINED SIMPLY REVISED 2ND EDITION

Library of Congress Cataloging-in-Publication Data

Vincent, Wendy M., 1975- author.
 The complete guide to growing healing and medicinal herbs : everything you need to know explained simply / by: Wendy Vincent. -- Revised 2nd edition.
    pages cm
Includes bibliographical references.
ISBN 978-1-62023-012-1 (alk. paper) -- ISBN 1-62023-012-7 (alk. paper)
1. Medicinal plants. 2. Herbs--Therapeutic use. I. Title.
SB293.V56 2015
615.3'21--dc23
                           2015022111

2ND EDITION EDITOR: Colleen McTiernan
ART DIRECTOR: Meg Buchner • megadesn@mchsi.com

Printed on Recycled Paper

Printed in the United States

Reduce. Reuse.
RECYCLE.

A decade ago, Atlantic Publishing signed the Green Press Initiative. These guidelines promote environmentally friendly practices, such as using recycled stock and vegetable-based inks, avoiding waste, choosing energy-efficient resources, and promoting a no-pulping policy. We now use 100-percent recycled stock on all our books. The results: in one year, switching to post-consumer recycled stock saved 24 mature trees, 5,000 gallons of water, the equivalent of the total energy used for one home in a year, and the equivalent of the greenhouse gases from one car driven for a year.

Over the years, we have adopted a number of dogs from rescues and shelters. First there was Bear and after he passed, Ginger and Scout. Now, we have Kira, another rescue. They have brought immense joy and love not just into our lives, but into the lives of all who met them.

We want you to know a portion of the profits of this book will be donated in Bear, Ginger and Scout's memory to local animal shelters, parks, conservation organizations, and other individuals and nonprofit organizations in need of assistance.

*– **Douglas & Sherri Brown**,*
President & Vice-President of Atlantic Publishing

Trademark Disclaimer

All trademarks, trade names, or logos mentioned or used are the property of their respective owners and are used only to directly describe the products being provided. Every effort has been made to properly capitalize, punctuate, identify, and attribute trademarks and trade names to their respective owners, including the use of® and ™ wherever possible and practical. Atlantic Publishing Group, Inc. is not a partner, affiliate, or licensee with the holders of said trademarks.

Dedication

*This book is dedicated to the generations of gardeners
who have come before me.*

Acknowledgments

I would like to thank my supportive circle of friends and family for encouraging me to reach for the stars. To my parents, who instilled in me a love of learning and books at an early age, and to my in-laws for so warmly welcoming me into their family many years ago. To my husband for his enduring love, encouragement, and support. And to my children, the next generation of dirty hands and green thumbs.

Disclaimer

This book is intended as a reference volume only, not as a medical manual. This book is for entertainment purposes and is meant to increase your knowledge of the latest developments in using herbs for medicinal purposes. The information given here is not intended as a substitute for any treatment that may have been prescribed by your doctor. Herbs and other natural care remedies are not substitutes for professional medical care. We urge you to seek the best medical resources available to help you make informed decisions. You should consult your physician or a physician with expertise in herbs before treating yourself with herbs or combining them with any medication. Women who are pregnant, may become pregnant, or are considering becoming pregnant should not use herbs or other medications without seeking the approval of their doctors. The information in this book is intended for adults, and you should consult your child's pediatrician before administering any herbal treatment to a child, especially one under the age of 2. If you suspect you have a medical problem, we urge you to seek competent medical help before taking herbal treatments.

Table of Contents

Chapter 9: Body Systems and Herbs to Promote Health 237

Chapter 10: Selling Healing Herbs 249

Final Thoughts 255

Appendix A : Additional Healing Recipes 257

Introduction

Historically, herbs have been grown not only for their ornamental and edible uses, but also for their healing and medicinal power. Throughout the centuries, herbs were grown to treat various ailments including toothaches, open wounds, the pains of childbirth, bronchitis, and digestive problems. Prior to written history, herbal folklore traditions for the medicinal uses of herbs were passed down from one generation to another through tightly guarded, familial oral histories and hands-on learning experiences. Each individual family, tribe, and civilization had its own herbal remedies based on custom and the medicinal plants that were locally available. Native American women, for example, would prepare a tea from the root of the cotton plant to alleviate problems associated with childbirth. Medicinally, the root of the cotton plant helps tighten the uterus and encourage regular menstruation after childbirth.

The combination of the written word with the explorative nature of the human spirit, however, has allowed cultures to assimilate herbal remedies from a wide range of backgrounds and historical uses into a readily available base of contemporary treatments. Naturopathic doctors, for instance, often use the ages-old remedy of stinging nettle to eliminate mucus in the treatment of coughs and allergies. Modern cultures around the world continue to incorporate ancient herbal healing traditions into their own medical treatments in an effort to improve the quality of life and triumph over illness.

Throughout history, cultures have relied on the wisdom of prior generations to learn how to use medicinal plants in healing. Examples of the significant role that herbs play throughout history can be found in a variety of cultures around the world. The Lascaux cave paintings in France that depict drawings of herbs are carbon dated back to somewhere between 25000 and 13000 B.C. One of the earliest written records of medicinal plants, dating back to the Ancient Egyptians, is the Ebers Papyrus of 1500 B.C. The document includes lists of dozens of medicinal plants, their specific uses, and related spells and incantations. The papyrus also suggests the existence of herbal doctors. Prior to the Ebers Papyrus, the Chinese Emperor Shen Nong (also known as Divine Farmer), circa 2737 B.C., was a well-known grower and practitioner of medicinal herbs. Credited with being the father of traditional Chinese herbal medicine, Shen Nong's beliefs of herbal remedies were put into use and passed down orally for generations. His thinking and practices were compiled around 220 A.D. into a written volume titled *Shen Nong Ben Cao Jing (Herbal Medicine Classic of Shen Nong)*. This text included hundreds of herbal medicines, laid the foundation for modern Chinese herbal medicine, and has been translated and incorporated into a variety of medicinal and herbal texts around the world. The advent of the written word, in correlation with the ability to travel beyond one's own village, led to the expansion of using a greater variety of healing plants for medicinal purposes.

By about the 2nd century B.C., trade routes for medicinal and culinary herbs became well traveled between Europe, India, Asia, and the Middle East. As people began to travel beyond their own villages, they learned more about the healing properties of different herbs. With a greater interest in new healing plants, the herb trade grew throughout the world, resulting in additional documentations of herbs and their uses. The Greek physician Dioscorides wrote the first illustrated herbal resource, *De Materia Medica*.

The book listed 600 herbs with almost 400 full-page color illustrations. Although the original text did not survive through the centuries, its contents have been preserved through a variety of copies and translations. As legend goes, the *De Materia Medica* was created for Juliana Anicia, daughter of the Roman Emperor Flavius Anicius Olybrius. This book was translated into many languages and used as the primary reference in Europe until about the 17th century A.D.

The enclosed monastic gardens of the monasteries in the Middle Ages provided their sheltered inhabitants with everything needed to sustain them, including a healing medicinal herbal garden. By combining the practical use of herbs as medicines alongside praying for divine intervention, monks were able to treat and cure common ailments. Herbs during the Middle Ages were also used to disguise the tastes of meats and other foods that were rotting, as well as body odor from infrequent bathing. The interest in growing medicinal herbs in Islamic cultures during the Middle Ages led to an establishment of medical schools that combined the medicinal knowledge of nearby Indian, Chinese, Greek, and European cultures. As a result, this study evolved into the science of pharmacology — the study of drugs, their uses, and their interactions.

Throughout history, herbs were grown for their healing properties to cleanse the body, cure common ailments, regulate the digestive system, and stimulate the immune system. By the 19th century, however, people no longer needed to grow herbs to use as domestic medications. Modern technologies allowed people to purchase synthetic substitutes of herbal remedies. Today, the pendulum is beginning to swing in the other direction, toward a renewed interest in a more holistic and natural approach to wellness. We are beginning to see a rise in backyard herbal gardens that include a variety of medicinal herbs. Growing a personal herb garden to heal basic ailments like burns or bug bites is becoming a popular hobby that has deep roots in ancient healing traditions.

This book is intended to be a step-by-step guide to learn about medicinal herbs and how to cultivate them in your own backyard. You will learn about the medicinal qualities of specific herbs, how to choose herbs based on your growing region, what type of soil and weather conditions they will thrive in, and how much water they require. In addition to learning how to grow a healthy, pest-free herb garden, you will learn how to harvest, store, and safely use herbs in various forms, including teas, tinctures, and salves.

Happy growing and healing!

Chapter 1

MEDICINES FROM THE EARTH

What is an Herb?

The term "herb" is derived from "herba," the Latin word for "grass." Originally, the term only referred to grasses, green crops and other leafy plants, but today an herb is considered to be any plant, tree, or shrub that is valued and utilized for its culinary, medicinal and aesthetic purposes. Belonging to any number of genera and species, herbs do not all have the same botanical characteristics. Each variety of herbs is distinctive in its makeup, yet they all have active parts that can affect various functions of the body. In addition to culinary uses, some herbs have properties to cure and prevent ailments.

Herbs can be annuals, biennials, or perennials. **Annuals** are started from seeds, grow, and then die in a one-year cycle. **Biennials** are plants that require two years to complete their life cycle. A **perennial** is a plant that has a top portion above the soil that dies back in the winter and comes back in the spring from the same roots. An herb can also be an **evergreen** — a plant with foliage that remains green throughout the year — or a tropical flower, such as an orchid. Some herbs, such as the dandelion, are considered weeds. A weed, however, is just an undesirable, sometimes even unattractive, plant that grows where gardeners do not want it to grow. A plant commonly viewed as a weed can, nonetheless, possess healing powers if used properly.

Oftentimes, unexpected natural plant matter, like weeds, can actually be considered an herbal healing remedy. Examples of nontraditional herbs might include the bark of the white willow tree, which is used as a pain reliever. Some medicinal herbs are also culinary herbs, such as ginger and thyme. Ginger relieves motion sickness, and thyme is often used for immune system support. Many plant-derived products are also considered healing herbal remedies. For example, the pollen bees collect from flowers can be considered an herb due to its nutritional and medicinal properties. Bee pollen can be used as a dietary supplement, as it contains a high level of protein (more than meat) to assist in maintaining proper bodily functions. Bee pollen can also reduce seasonal allergy symptoms. It is readily available at a variety of health food stores. Honey has the ability to heal as well because it helps the body retain calcium. In addition, honey also helps heal kidney and liver disorders, poor circulation, and colds. Because honey is produced from a wide variety of plants and plant nectars, it is also helpful in battling seasonal allergies. A spoonful of locally produced honey will help your body build up an immunity to seasonal allergies and decrease the severity of allergy symptoms.

Other plant-related products that may fall into the herbal category are nuts, seeds, hulls, shells, berries, plant oils and saps. Barley, brown rice, wheat and oats provide our bodies with the proper nutrients needed for human growth. Pumpkin seeds, sunflower seeds, nuts, and soybeans contain high levels of proteins that strengthen our bodies. Seeds, nuts and grains provide lecithin and vitamins A, B, C, and F, and they are a healthy source of unsaturated fatty acids. In addition, seeds, nuts and grains contain auxones, a natural substance that prevents premature aging through cell renewal. Seeds also contain pacifarins, which help build up antibiotic responses and increase our natural resistance to disease.

Some plants that are classified as vegetables can also be considered herbs. Garlic, for example, is one of the best-known vegetables that also falls into the herb category. Not only does it add aromatic flavoring to foods, garlic also offers antibiotic properties, blood purifying abilities, and cholesterol-lowering capabilities. Celery is another vegetable that has a long history of being used as a medicinal herb. Celery seeds are commonly used to rid the body of uric acid, which causes inflammation and pain in people who have gout and arthritis. Celery seeds also promote restfulness.

Herbs provide certain antioxidant properties that are helpful to our bodies. **Antioxidants** are believed to delay and prevent damage to cells that free radicals cause. **Free radicals** are damaging by-products that are created when cells use the crucial oxygen they need. Free radicals can form in a variety of ways. For example, being exposed to outside conditions like pollution, alcohol, drugs and pesticides speed up the production of free radicals. Poor diets, radiation and prolonged sun exposure can also increase free radical production. Unfortunately, the free radical by-products can cause damage to our bodies.

Antioxidants find and destroy free radicals, preventing and repairing the damage free radicals cause. Heart disease, diabetes, macular degeneration and cancer are all contributed to oxidative damage from free radicals. Several vitamins and minerals are antioxidants, and antioxidants are also made within cells. In addition to vitamins, minerals and cellular antioxidants, there are other essential antioxidants that must come from your diet, including herbs. Herbs are plants that are easily recognized by your body as a food source. Because of this, your body is able to use these nutrients from herbs in a natural way to benefit the body.

Some examples of antioxidants include flavonoids and tannins. **Flavonoids** are plant compounds with antioxidant properties that benefit your health. In addition to having antiviral and anti-allergic properties, flavonoids are also thought to protect against inflammation and tumor growth. **Tannins**, on the other hand, are a type of plant compound that exerts high antioxidant activity and offers protection for the gastrointestinal system. The term "tannin" comes from its original use in tanning leathers. It is thought that the existence of tannins in some herbs can help relieve gastrointestinal complaints like diarrhea. The properties of flavonoids and tannins can lower the risk of cardiovascular disease and cancer.

Why Grow Herbs?

There are many reasons to have a personal herb garden, including medicinal, culinary, and purely decorative. An added bonus to growing your own herbs is the benefits for your personal health and well-being. Growing your own botanical medicines is fun and exciting as well as beneficial to the welfare of the earth. Medicinal herbs are perhaps the oldest form of health care known to man. Recently, gardeners and novices alike are rediscovering the magic and pleasure of growing their own healing herbs in pursuit of re-awakening ancient medicinal customs.

Following centuries-old traditions, growing your own herbs can be a rewarding hobby. Not only do herbs make a pretty and fragrant addition to any yard or windowsill, but there is also a pleasure derived from growing, harvesting and creating your own home remedies. Getting started does not require a large financial commitment or any specialized skills. With some knowledge, interest in the benefits of herbs and a little patience, it is easy to embark on your own herbal adventure.

Gardening provides physical exercise and private time for meditative contemplation. Some of the health-related benefits of gardening include an increase in mobility and flexibility, a decrease in blood pressure and strength training. You will also have the advantage of having fresh herbs on hand to use in home remedies and recipes. Also, you will know exactly what went into the growth and care of your plants and you will be able to avoid harsh chemicals that are traditionally used in commercial growing.

CASE STUDY

Rosemari Roast, owner
Walk in the Woods, LLC
http://walkinthewoods.byregion.net
860-480-3642

"I am dedicated to returning the People's Medicine back into the hands of the people."

Rosemari Roast is an herbalist, healer, and artist who has studied herbalism and earned national board certification through the American Association of Drugless Practitioners. Additionally, she continues to engage in learning experiences at every opportunity and considers herself primarily self-taught. Her humble view stems from a belief that experience is really the only true teacher. After all, she feels, we have different experiences, even working with the same botanicals, and all experiences are of value and meaning to every individual. All are valid in some way.

In addition to personal consultations, classes, workshops and lectures, Roast offers weed walks, eclectic healing sessions, and more. Weed walks provide students with the opportunities to learn about edible and healing plants that are commonly referred to as "weeds." Through sharing her experiences with others, Roast teaches one-on-one and within groups. This teaching involves gaining an understanding of the nutritional, medicinal, and holistic benefits of the plant realm, allowing people a capacity to make their own green recommendations for wellness. To her, herbalism is truly a medicine of the people, and exploring this realm and applying its wisdom is empowering and allows for individuals to take back some of the power that modern life hides from them — and in some cases has attempted to strip away. She often quotes the words credited to Hippocrates, the father of Western medicine: "Let food be thy medicine and medicine be thy food."

Roast's connection to nature runs deep. She is a long-time gardener and strives to grow much of her own food. It was more than 30 years ago, when she started to employ organic methods, that the green world really opened up to her. Roast started growing comfrey *(symphytum x. uplandicum)* to add to her compost and mulch for its nutritive qualities. It was that experience that inspired Roast to take a deep and conscious look into the hidden gifts — for the garden and herself — of the green world.

Roast grows herbs primarily for personal use and for use in teaching. She does make some products with fresh plant matter, and dries some as well, which are available for sale. She sells most items directly to her students and clients, while a few simple herbal products are available at online shops ArtFire and Etsy.

To get started with healing and medicinal hers, Roast offers the following tips:

- Get to know what's already growing around you, in your gardens and lawns, even if you perceive them as weeds.

- Network in your area to find other herbalists and growers. Connecting with other herby people can help in identifying botanicals and their wellness value.

- Trading perennials with other growers is a way to expand your gardens while learning and making new friends.

Roast suggests growing the following herbs:

- Nettle for its spectacular nutritional value.

- Garlic for its delicious preventive and healing qualities.

- Violets for their holistic soothing verve, internally and externally.

- Sage for its calming abilities.

- Burdock for its strong, nutritional, cleansing energies.

- Lemon balm for its simple, calming and curative properties (and it makes a nice ale, too). Plus, these options have diverse uses, from fresh food to tinctures, water, vinegar, and oil infusions to mead, ales, crafts, and so much more.

Healing herbs can also provide an alternative to modern-day synthetic drug use. Synthetic medications are created by mixing together chemical compounds in a laboratory or factory setting. Conventional medicine, although originally derived from healing plants, strays from its natural origins. The bark and leaves of the willow tree, for example, were originally used to relieve pain and reduce fever. Instead of using the natural leaves and bark, modern-day aspirin is recreated synthetically in a laboratory to achieve the same pain-relieving results. Today, more people are questioning the heavy use of pharmaceuticals and taking charge of their own health and well-being by learning a bit of the age-old wisdom of herbs and more natural approaches to wellness. By growing your own healing herbs, you will be able to contribute positively to your own health, as well as the health of your entire family. *Refer to the Appendix A for a sample of recipes to implement the healing herbs that you grow yourself.*

The Different Properties of Herbs

Herbs are extremely versatile plants. One herb can be utilized as a treatment for several ailments because it contains several compounds with different healing properties. For instance, white willow bark, because it contains the natural chemical glucoside salicin, is an effective painkiller. Glucoside salicin was the first form of aspirin and is now chemically reproduced. On the other hand, willow is also known as a very effective antiseptic and a sedative.

Herbs have many healing actions. Some herbs have antibiotic properties, while others are antiseptic, anti-inflammatory, anesthetic, or antiviral. Others are decongestants, diuretics, immune system stimulants, or laxatives. For example, American Indians used St. John's wort to treat tuberculosis and other breathing ailments. Because of its antibacterial and antiviral properties, St. John's wort is also very useful for treating bacterial and viral infections. These same properties have also been found useful in removing phlegm from the chest and lungs. Interestingly enough, some recent research independently conducted at the Weizmann Institute of Science in Israel and at New York University shows that hypercin and pseudohypercin, elements of St. John's wort, may inhibit the growth of retroviruses like HIV.

Healing Actions Defined

Anesthetic: An agent that temporarily slows down neuron function and creates a loss of sensation.

Antibacterial: Inhibits or destroys the growth of bacteria.

Antibiotic: Prevents the growth of microorganisms that cause infectious diseases.

Antifungal: Inhibits and destroys growth of fungi.

Anti-inflammatory: Reduces or suppresses inflammation.

Antiparasitic: Combats parasite activity.

Antiseptic: Prevents infection by killing microorganisms.

Antiviral: Eliminates or inhibits the effects of viruses.

Decongestant: A treatment that relieves congestion.

Diuretic: Increases the excretion of urine.

Immune System Stimulate: Helps support the immune system in protecting against illness.

Laxative: Relieves constipation.

Painkiller: A medicine that relieves pain.

Sedative: Calms and soothes nervousness, irritation, or anxiety.

Another healing herb is the common dandelion, which is a well-known diuretic. Dandelions are easily consumable as a salad green or can be used in a tea. Rich in potassium, it supports the body's vital potassium levels, rather than depleting those levels as many pharmaceutical diuretics do. Potassium, which the kidneys regulate, is one of the most important minerals in the body, and it helps eliminate excess sodium. In fact, potassium and sodium work together in the body to regulate the amount of water moving in and out of the cells. Dandelion is also great for weight loss because it increases the flow of urine and acts as a gentle laxative. Because it is high in potassium and organic sodium, dandelion is a great balancer of electrolytes and offers lots of vitamin A. Dandelion greens contain 7,000 units of vitamin A per ounce, compared with lettuce, which offers 1,200 units per ounce, and carrots, which offer 1,275 units per ounce. Vitamin A helps the body's cells reproduce normally and also helps boost white blood cells and supports the function of the thyroid. The thyroid takes iodine, found in many foods that we ingest, and converts it into thyroid hormones. Thyroid hormonal function is crucial for regulating how quickly the body uses energy, makes proteins, and regulates hormones throughout the body.

CASE STUDY
Practitioner of oriental medicine

"Where I'm from, it is said if you are ill, look in your garden. The herb that keeps growing in your garden is likely to be the herb that you may need to improve your health."

This practitioner of oriental medicine was first exposed to locally grown medicinal herbs in his hometown. As a practitioner of oriental medicine, he uses medicinal Chinese herbs with an understanding of how they can affect the body on an energetic and physical level. For example, he believes that herbs that grow during certain seasons of the year often have medicinal properties to treat a particular season's illness. Echinacea is ready to be harvested in the fall, for instance, just in time to build up immunity for cold and flu season. What he does not treat with acupuncture for his patients, he is able to treat through the use of Chinese and Western medicinal herbs.

He feels that growing your own medicinal herbs has many benefits. "When you are involved in planting and growing your own herbs, this allows your plants to become familiar with you and adjust to your energetic field, thereby creating a synergistic relationship between you and your plants," he said. Through his experiences in growing and working with medicinal herbs, he recommends that you do your research to learn how to grow, harvest, and store herbs properly. He warns that all herbs have a safe dosage that should be respected for healing. A larger dosage, for example, does not mean better or faster results and could, in fact, be dangerous. He recommends that you always take the suggested dosage and always consult with an herbal practitioner.

When choosing herbs to grow in a personal herbal garden, he suggest the following herbs for their medicinal uses: sage, green onions, rosemary, parsley, aloe vera, peppermint, celery, Melissa leaves (lemon balm), chamomile, lettuce, and fennel.

Some of his favorite recipes and uses for healing herbs include:

- **Colds:** At the first stages of a cold, prior to a fever setting in (when you are experiencing chills, headache, aversion to cold/wind, and a stiff neck), combine 6 to 9 grams of fresh ginger, three green onions, and one cinnamon stick in a pot and bring it to a boil. Let it boil for two to five minutes and then let the mixture sit for a few minutes. Add 1 to 2 tablespoons of raw unfiltered honey. Drink three cups of this mixture a day. This is a diaphoretic recipe, which means that it will cause you to perspire heavily. As such, avoid being exposed to drafts.

- **Immune system support:** Add 1 tablespoon of echinacea to 1 cup of warm water one to two times a day.

- **Poor digestion:** Use 1 tablespoon fennel seeds per cup of boiling water after meals.

- **Muscle relaxer:** Use 1 tablespoon of chamomile flower per cup of boiling water.

- **Insomnia:** Use 1 tablespoon Melissa leaf (lemon balm) per cup of boiling water before going to bed.

- **Burns:** Apply the gel of aloe vera topically to burns or any kind of skin condition.

Additionally, there are many herbs that are considered to have antibiotic properties. Garlic is a well-known culinary and medicinal herb and is also a powerful antibiotic. It is active against Staphylococcus aureus (the cause of staph infections), Candida albicans (yeast infection of the mouth), E. coli, and Pseudomonas aeruginosa (a bacteria that can cause a variety of illnesses in humans and animals), to name a few. Garlic is also antibacterial, antiviral, antiseptic, antiparasitic and antifungal.

Honey is another herbal remedy and contains a complex assortment of enzymes, trace minerals, organic acids, antibiotic agents and hormones. It also contains vitamin C, vitamin A, beta-carotene, the complete complex of B vitamins, vitamin D, vitamin E and vitamin K. Many herbs, such as astragalus, boneset and ginseng, are well known for strengthening the immune system.

Migraine headaches are debilitating, and many people suffer from them. Feverfew is the optimal herb for diminishing migraines. At times, doctors advise their patients to take feverfew if pharmaceuticals have no effect. Feverfew prevents migraines over time because it has an anti-inflammatory effect. In Europe, it is common for a migraine sufferer to take feverfew by placing three or four leaves on a sandwich. It has been shown that the leaves of feverfew are more effective as a healing agent when they are used fresh rather than dried.

There are hundreds of classified healing and medicinal herbs, and this book will highlight a portion of them, based on usefulness and ease of growing. Remedy suggestions this book will offer include: herbal antacids, fever reducers, herbs for cuts and burns, anti-inflammatory herbs for joints and muscles, diuretics to rid the body of excess water, and herbs for indigestion. As with all pharmaceuticals, one herb might work better for one part of the body than for another. In addition, one may be more effective for one person than for another. It is helpful to know the potential benefits of each herb to decide which herbs to grow in your own garden.

Common Ailments and Herbs for Treating Them

When used properly, herbs can be an effective tool in treating a variety of common ailments. Some ways in which herbs can be used medicinally are as an infusion, tincture, or decoction. An **infusion** is created when herbs are soaked or boiled in water. A **decoction** is a stronger and more concentrated version of an infusion. Herbal **tinctures**, on the other hand, are made by steeping herbs in alcohol or vinegar. *Additional details about creating infusions, tinctures, and decoctions will follow in Chapter 8.* By using herbs to create infusions, tinctures and decoctions, you can treat some common ailments at home.

The following is by no means a complete list, but rather a quick guide to some common ailments herbs can remedy.

Ailment	Herbal Remedy
Acne	Basil oil, witch hazel, tea tree oil (diluted)
Arthritis	Angelica, boneset, cayenne, meadowsweet, white willow
Asthma	Anise, coltsfoot, ginger
Bronchitis	Echinacea, garlic
Burns	Aloe vera
Cholesterol — high	Alfalfa, cayenne, fenugreek, garlic
Colds and flu	Echinacea, ginger, hyssop
Colic	Dill, slippery elm
Conjunctivitis	Barberry, eyebright
Constipation	Buckthorn, Cascara sagrada, psyllium, senna

Cough	Anise, coltsfoot, eucalyptus, fenugreek, horehound, licorice, wild cherry
Diarrhea	Bayberry, blackberry, goldenseal
Dizziness	Ginger
Ear infection	Echinacea
Emphysema	Coltsfoot, thyme
Fever	Black haw, ginger, meadowsweet, white willow
Gas	Peppermint, dill
Gout	Nettle
Gum disease	Chaparral, myrrh
Halitosis	Parsley, alfalfa
Hay fever	Local honey, nettle
Headache	Feverfew, cayenne
High blood pressure	Cayenne, ginkgo, hawthorn
Hemorrhoids	Witch hazel
Herpes	Comfrey, echinacea, hyssop
Hives	Parsley
Insomnia	Motherwort, skullcap, valerian
Menopausal discomforts	Black cohosh, fennel, red clover
Menstrual discomfort	Black cohosh, fennel, red clover, yarrow
Menstruation (heavy)	Cayenne, shepherd's purse
Morning sickness	Ginger, mints
Motion sickness	Ginger

Nausea	Ginger
Pain	Black haw, cayenne, meadowsweet, white willow
Psoriasis	Echinacea, gotu kola
Sore throat	Fenugreek, licorice, mullein, sage
Stress	Catnip, chamomile, motherwort, skullcap, yarrow
Tinnitus (ringing in the ears)	Ginkgo
Toothache	Cloves
Urinary incontinence	Cranberry
Urinary tract infection	Cranberry, uva ursi
Varicose veins	Gotu kola
Wound healing	Aloe, comfrey, echinacea, eucalyptus, slippery elm, yarrow
Yeast infection	Chamomile, cinnamon, dandelion, echinacea

Precautions

Please note that herbs are powerful, and any plant that can help can also harm if not used properly. Belladonna, for example, if used properly can be an effective muscle relaxer and sedative. If used at full strength, belladonna, also known as deadly nightshade, can cause death. To use medicinal herbs, it is extremely important to educate yourself about herbs and your health condition. If you do have questions while using herbal remedies, consult with a good herbalist, or naturopathic doctor in your area. An **herbalist**, or herbal practitioner, is someone who is specially trained in herbal medicine and uses plants and other natural substances to prevent and treat illness and improve health and healing. A **naturopathic doctor** is a primary care doctor trained in treating the whole person through the use of natural methods to prevent and treat disease. A naturopathic doctor will perform regular physical exams and often works as part of a team with traditional medical doctors for testing and treatment purposes. You can ask at your herb or health food store, check the yellow pages, or search online for a good herbalist or naturopathic doctor for assistance with treating a medical condition. The American Association of Naturopathic Physicians provides a directory of doctors by city and state at **www.naturopathic.org**. Be sure to inform your doctor and pharmacist of any herbs you are taking, as herbal remedies can interact with prescription drugs. When used properly, herbs rid the body of offending pathogens and support weak body systems, allowing the body to get back to maximum health. Herbs can work with the body to balance the its natural processes.

Are herbs considered completely safe? As with any pharmaceuticals and over-the-counter medications, too much of something is still too much. Herbs, just as with anything else, should be taken in suggested dosages, starting with the lowest dosage if you have never taken it before. Many people believe herbs are safer than pharmaceuticals purely because they are natural, while critics of herbal medications feel pharmaceuticals are safer because the dosage is more regulated and herb users must guess at the dosages they take.

The potency of a particular herb depends on many things: the plant's genetics, the herb's growing conditions, the maturity of the plant, the method of preparation and the length of time the herb has been in storage. However, no one can guarantee that prescription drugs are used in the manner intended either.

Below are some guidelines to follow when using medicinal herbs:

- With the exception of a few, herbs should not be given to children under the age of 2 — and even then you need to dilute the infusion. *This will be covered further in later chapters.*

- If you have not taken an herb previously, start with the lowest dosage, particularly if you are over 65.

- With the exception of a few herbs, pregnant and nursing women should not use medicinal herbs. Even if the herb is acceptable to use when pregnant, you should still consult a physician or specialist first.

- If you are on chronic pharmaceuticals, use extra caution because herbs can interact with the medications you are taking. For example, an herbal remedy may counteract the effectiveness of birth control pills. Do not take herbs at the same time you take your prescription drugs, and always consult with your doctor or a naturopathic physician.

- If you have any signs of toxicity, stop taking the herb immediately. Signs of toxicity can include nausea, diarrhea, upset stomach, dizziness, or headache.

- When growing your own herbs, be sure to identify an herb correctly.

- Do not use herbs indiscriminately, but with wisdom and knowledge.

NOTE: This book is not intended to diagnose or prescribe. Just because an herb is known to help others with a particular ailment does not mean it will work for you or that it will not produce adverse side effects when you take the herb. This book lists common herbs that have the potential to enhance your life and improve your health along with exercise, proper diet and a healthy mental attitude.

Chapter 2

THYME
BEGAN IN A GARDEN

Before embarking on your herbal garden adventure, a little planning goes a long way. Planning ahead will keep your project organized, limit frustration, and ensure that the journey of learning to grow your own healing herbs is an enjoyable experience. Key considerations while planning a healing herb garden include:

- Determining which growing zone you are located in.

- Matching the growing habits of specific herbs to the weather and soil conditions as dictated by your region for optimal growing results.

- Figuring out which herbs will work best for you based your on needs and planting conditions, as well as the best herbs to plant together for mutual benefit.

- Deciding where you are going to plant your garden.

- Choosing your planting conditions and methods — indoor versus outdoors, containers versus beds, or a combination of choices.

One way to begin the planning process and organize a future garden is to use a three-ring binder. A three-ring binder provides one location to store all of your notes, garden plans, shopping and to-do lists, pictures, and seed packets. It also allows you the flexibility to add or remove items throughout the process as your garden develops. Any type of binder that you already have at home will work, or you could purchase one at a store that sells office supplies.

Dividers or category tags might also come in handy to create different sections in the binder and make searching easier. Divider tags are available at any number of stores that sell office supplies. The different sections might include:

- Zone and Soil Conditions
- Garden Layout Ideas
- Articles
- Notes
- To Do / To Buy
- Herb Information

Lunar Gardening

The practice of **lunar gardening**, or gardening by the cycles of the moon, is an ancient wisdom that continues on through the traditions and practices of gardeners today. The well-known *Farmer's Almanac* is a famous example of a gardening guide that relies on nature's cycles for its predictions. Planting, caring for and harvesting based on the cycles of the moon and nature's own rhythms, will create healthier and more productive plants in an herbal healing garden. The moon's gravitational pull on underground water tables affects the moisture level in the soil that is available to the plants for nourishment. Additionally, the level of moonlight available during the growing season will also affect seed germination.

Cycles of the Moon

New Moon	Waxing	Full	Waning
The gravitational pull of the new moon draws water upward, providing additional nourishment at the surface of the ground for seeds and plants.	The moonlight is increasingly stronger, but the gravitational pull lessens. This creates strong leaf growth.	The gravitational pull draws down instead of up, pulling more moisture into the roots of the plants. The light also begins to decrease after the full moon.	Both the gravitational pull and moonlight decrease into a resting period.
This is the best time to plant above-ground annuals like celery and basil.	The waxing moon is the best time for planting just prior to the full moon. Annuals with interior seeds like pumpkins should be planted.	This is the ideal time for planting tap roots like onions, garlic and dill.	The waning moon, or fourth quarter, is the ideal time to cultivate, harvest, transplant and prune.

To start planning an herbal garden, begin researching and gathering information specific to your needs. Gardening magazines, the Internet, libraries and local garden centers can provide you with a wealth of information to get started. Cut out or copy pictures from magazines and books of garden designs and layouts that would work in your yard and include them in the garden layout ideas section of the planning binder. Start a preliminary list of herbs that interest you so that you can begin researching their specific needs and growing conditions. *See Chapter 3 for some suggestions on healing herbs to grow.* Make a list of nearby nurseries, garden centers and local colleges that might offer seminars and classes with local experts to gain insightful knowledge. The binder can become a useful planning and informational tool in growing a healing garden.

With your binder in hand, it is time to get started on the detailed planning process for your herbal healing garden to determine your specific growing conditions.

Determining your Zone

The first significant detail in planning a garden is to determine which herbs will grow in your zone. A **growing zone** is a geographically determined area that defines which category of plants will be able to grow in a specific region. The zone considers climate-related conditions like minimum temperatures a plant can withstand. The U.S. Department of Agriculture (USDA) originally developed the various hardiness zones in the United States, and these zones continue to be the standard today. **Hardiness** refers to the average minimum low temperature a plant can survive in as a perennial. Use the hardiness zones as a guideline rather than the rule because the hardiness of an individual plant depends on several factors, including the temperature range for any given year and the pH level of the soil. For example, if the plant is protected from the wind and elements by a wall, shrubs, or trees, this will also make a difference. An updated map of the USDA hardiness zones can be found at **http://planthardiness.ars.usda.gov/PHZMWeb**. For example, if you are located in the state of West Virginia, your hardiness growing zone could be anywhere from 5a to 7a.

To determine if a particular herb will do well in your growing zone, find out that plant's hardiness zone. The tag included with the plant at the nursery or the back of a seed package will show the best zone an herb will grow in. If the seed packet does not have a USDA hardiness zone map on the back, there still will be instructions for growing that particular herb. If you are buying plants from a nearby nursery, be assured that those plants will grow in your zone because nurseries do not usually sell herbs that will not grow where they are sold.

Choosing Your Herbs

Plan a healing herb garden to suit your personal tastes, style and needs. When choosing the plants for the garden, be sure to consider which herbs you will use the most, which herbs grow best in your region, the location and condition of where they will be planted, and which herbs make good growing companions. *Refer to Appendix B for a quick reference list of healing herbs with the individual light preference, moisture level, pH preference and best method of starting.*

Choosing Herbs for Extreme Climates

Herbs are easy to grow in a variety of different climate locations. There are, however, areas where certain climatic conditions can prove to be challenging. In addition to soil condition, for example, it may be necessary to take into consideration a way in which to shelter or protect your garden from harsher climates in coastal, cool and wet, or hot and dry regions.

If you live near a beach, the salty sea air and winds can damage many herbs. To help better protect the plants, a planted hedge can act as a windbreak. Useful hedge plants like juniper *(Juniperus communis)* or rosemary can be planted tightly together to form a protective barrier. Plant your herbs within this barrier hedge with well-composted and mulched soil. Additionally, some herbs that perform particularly well in a coastal climate are those of Mediterranean origins like lavender and fennel.

For regions with a climate that is cool and wet, you should ideally choose medicinal plants that do well in or close to water. Moisture-loving plants include angelica, mint and valerian. Herbs that will perform in hot and dry climates, on the other hand, include bay, sage, oregano, dill and cilantro.

When choosing plants for the garden, choose herbs that you know you will use. For example, if you are prone to headaches, plant feverfew, fenugreek, or thyme. Likewise, if you suffer from heartburn, plant peppermint. This is your personal medicinal garden, so plant the healing herbs you will use most. Start with some of the easiest to grow and most useful herbs, but also be willing to experiment with new herbs every year to add to the further enjoyment of your herb garden.

You can also choose your garden according to which herbs you may want to use in the kitchen in addition to their healing properties. Fresh culinary herbs are wonderful to have on hand, and while you may not have considered any of them to be medicinal, many of them are. Thyme, for instance, can be used in an infusion to settle the stomach, and parsley can sweeten your breath and will also help condition dry hair. Many herbs, such as lavender, have a wonderful fragrance that soothes and calms. For example, a small lavender pillow tucked inside your pillowcase is wonderful for ensuring sweet dreams.

When deciding which herbs to plant, you should also consider the physical location of the herb garden. Sunlight, for example, is very important. Check whether your garden site is in full sun, partial shade, or shade by observing how much sun it receives during the day. A garden location with at least six hours of direct sunlight is considered **full sun**. **Partial shade** indicates that a garden receives only three to six hours of direct sunlight during the day, and a garden location that receives less than three hours of sunlight is considered **shade**. In addition, some herbs prefer dry soil, while others thrive in moist soil. Try to group herbs according to soil, light, pH and water requirements. The pH of the soil will be an important determining factor when figuring out which herbs will grow best in your yard. *Soil pH will be discussed in Chapter 4.* Most herbs do love full sun, but there are those that require shade.

CASE STUDY

Rose Fogg, greenhouse grower
Ginger Brook Herbs
www.herbfestct.com
mooncat13@yahoo.com

Rose Fogg is an independent greenhouse grower who sells and provides herbs to a variety of vendors throughout the state of Connecticut. According to Fogg, she has been "growing forever" and is as enthusiastic about her herb plants as parents are about their newborn child. One of the places Fogg proudly displays and sells her "babies" is at the annual Connecticut HerbFest.

The HerbFest is sponsored yearly by the Connecticut Herb Association (**www.ctherb.org**). It is a family-friendly event that offers workshops, demonstrations, lectures, herb walks, entertainment, food and family-related activities. The fest, according to its organizers, is a celebration of useful herbs and our connection to the earth.

In addition to the annual HerbFest, Fogg sells her herb plants at farmers markets and other herb-related festivals and events alongside Ginger Brook Herbs. Kathy O'Kanos of Ginger Brook Herbs uses herbs to create healing blends. When asked about growing herbs, O'Kanos politely refers any questions to Fogg as the expert grower.

According to Fogg, some helpful tips on the best conditions for growing herbs from her years of experience include:

- Let the herbs get lots of sunlight.
- Pay careful attention to watering. There is a fine balance between too much and not enough.
- If a plant seems stressed, make changes.
- Look at each plant as an individual.
- Good drainage and composting is key in creating a good soil condition.

Light Preferences of Herbs

Many plants will only thrive in the right lighting conditions. Other herbs may tolerate a range of lighting conditions, but may not grow to their full potential if not planted in their preferred conditions. Herbs with similar light preferences make good companion plants to be planted together.

Here are some healing herbs listing according to their light preferences:

For a complete list of lighting preferences for healing herbs mentioned in this book, refer to the chart in Appendix B.

Prefer Full Sun	Tolerate Full Sun	Prefer Shade	Tolerate Shade	Prefer Partial Shade	Tolerate Partial Shade
Aloe	Angelica	Goldenseal	Angelica	Angelica	Anise hyssop
Anise	Bee balm	Hops	Lemon balm	Bee balm	Calendula
Basil	Mints	Passionflower	Mints	Mints	Catnip
Borage	Violet		Parsley	Violet	Chamomile
Calendula			Violet		Chives
Catnip					Cilantro

Prefer Full Sun	Tolerate Full Sun	Prefer Shade	Tolerate Shade	Prefer Partial Shade	Tolerate Partial Shade
Cayenne					Comfrey
Chamomile					Fennel
Chives					Feverfew
Cilantro					Hyssop
Cinnamon					Lemon balm
Comfrey					Marjoram
Corn					Rosemary
Dill					Woodruff
Echinacea					Tarragon
Fennel					Thyme
Feverfew					Wormwood
Flaxseed					
Garlic					
Hibiscus					
Hyssop					
Lavender					
Lemon					
Lemongrass					
Lemon balm					
Lemon Verbena					
Oregano					
Parsley					
Rosemary					
Sage					
Tarragon					
Thyme					
Wormwood					

Soil Moisture Preferences of Herbs

One of the secrets to growing healthy herbs is planting them in their preferred soil moisture level. Good soil drainage is essential to all healthy herbs. Regardless of whether the herb requires a high level of moisture, it still needs proper drainage. To test the drainage in your garden, dig a hole that is about 6 inches wide by 18 inches deep and set a measuring stick in the hole. Fill the hole with water and allow it to drain completely. This will usually take a full day or so. Once the hole has completely drained, fill the hole again to the top with water and measure hourly to see how quickly the water drains away. If it drains at the rate of less than ½ inch per hour, the soil is considered poor draining. If the rate is somewhere between ½ to 1 inch per hour, the drainage is slow, but still acceptable. Ideally, if the soil drains at the rate of 1 to 4 inches per hour, most plants will grow well in it. To improve the drainage in your garden, work sand or small pebbles 8 to 10 inches in the soil.

When planting, herbs that prefer the same type of soil moisture make good companion plants to be grouped together in the same growing beds. Here is a list of some soil preferences for healing herbs mentioned in this book:

For a complete list of moisture preferences for healing herbs mentioned in this book, refer to the chart in Appendix B.

Prefer Moist Soil	Prefer Moderately Moist Soil	Prefer Dry Soil
Basil	Anise hyssop	Aloe
Bee balm	Angelica	Anise
Calendula	Borage	Astragalus
Comfrey	Catnip	California poppy
Lemon balm	Chives	Caraway
Lemongrass	Dill	Chamomile
Lovage	Elecampane	Cilantro
Mints	Fennel	Feverfew
Nasturtium	Hops	Hyssop
Parsley	Lemon verbena	Lavender
Violet		Milk thistle
		Oregano
		Rosemary
		Sage
		Tarragon
		Thyme
		Wormwood

Herbs should be planted in soil with added organic matter to improve drainage and texture. The garden will benefit by choosing a location that gets sun most of the day and does not collect water after a heavy rain. It may be helpful to begin making lists of herbs that you would like to plant, then group them by light and soil conditions to determine the optimal location in your yard for planting.

Herbal Planting Companions

Some herbs make nice companion plants to other herbs, as well as vegetable plants, as they tolerate similar growing conditions. In addition, some herbs provide assistance to each other to improve growth and repel pests. Growing healing herbs in your garden will not only provide medicinal assistance to you and your family, but to your other plants as well.

Here is a list of herbs and some beneficial companions you can plant them with:

Herb	Plant with	Benefits
Anise	Basil	Increases essential oil in basil
Basil	Tomatoes, peppers	Improves growth and flavor; repels flies, mosquitoes
Bee balm	Tomatoes	Improves growth and flavor; attracts bees for pollination
Black-eyed Susan	Feverfew, hyssop, licorice	Repels insects; attracts birds
Borage	Strawberries, cucumbers	Attracts honeybees and repels a wide range of pests
Calendula	Anywhere in garden	Keeps nematodes out of soil; deters many pests
Catnip	Any plant	Repels flea beetles
Chamomile	Basil, wheat, cabbage, onion	Increases oil production; improves flavor
Cilantro	Spinach	Repels aphids, beetles, spider mites
Chives	Apple trees, broccoli, tomatoes, cabbage	Repels cabbage worms, aphids; deters deer
Dill	Corn, lettuce, cucumbers, onions	Repels aphids, spider mites

Herb	Plant with	Benefits
Fennel	Dill	Attracts ladybugs, which eat many harmful garden pests; repels aphids *Do not plant fennel with any other plant besides dill as fennel tends to kill all plants. Dill is the only exception.
Garlic	Peas, celery, cucumbers, lettuce	Repels aphids, ants; deters rabbits
Horseradish	Potatoes	Repels potato bugs
Hyssop	Cabbage	Repels cabbage moth larvae; attracts honeybees, butterflies
Mint	Cabbage, tomatoes	Repels cabbage moths; improves health of tomatoes
Nasturtiums	Radishes, tomatoes, cabbage, cucumbers	Repels aphids, other pests
Rosemary	Sage, beans, cabbage	Repels bean beetles, cabbage flies
Sage	Rosemary, beans, cabbage	Repels cabbage flies, cabbage looper; attracts honeybees, butterflies
Tarragon	Anything	Adds flavor to other plants; enhances growth; almost all pests dislike the scent
Wormwood	Throughout garden	Deters animals when planted as a border

Regardless of the herbs you decide to plant, you can take pride in knowing that you planted these herbs, you worked in your garden, and most importantly, you and your family will benefit from these wonderful gifts from nature. You will also learn about the interconnectedness of different plants and how they all benefit each other.

Garden Location and Style

There are a variety of ways to grow herbs, and the best way to decide on a growing method is to consider your lifestyle and space limitations. For example, if you only have a windowsill to dedicate to your project, you can still reap the benefits of herbs by planting a container garden directly on your windowsill. A healing herb garden can be planted as a container garden, in a raised bed, as in-ground fields, or as a combination of all three.

Container gardening

If space is limited, or you would like to start during winter when the danger of frost is present, consider **container gardening**, which entails growing a plant in a pot instead of directly sowing it in the ground. If you can fill the container with soil and allow proper drainage, you can grow herbs in almost anything. Some unusual containers you can use in container gardening include an old boot, enamel dishes, a fish tank, a bag of soil, or even a plastic storage container. Such choices maximize your small space, add interest to your garden and also create easy access to your plants. An herbal container garden right outside your kitchen makes adding a dash of basil or rosemary to your meals easy. A container garden requires considerably less maintenance than a raised bed or directly sown garden and is ideal for those who may not have enough space for a conventional garden.

Advantages to growing herbs in containers include the following:

- You can move the containers if your area experiences harsh weather.

- You do not have to worry about invasive plants and weeds.

- You can adapt your garden plan depending on the amount of space available.

- Containers offer more possibilities for the types of plants you can use and where you can plant them.

- Plants that are not hardy outside in winter can easily be moved indoors.

- You can control the type of soil the plant grows in.

Some important considerations when growing in containers include:

- Plants in containers will need additional fertilizing.

- Container plants need more frequent watering because they cannot draw moisture from the earth.

- Plants may need to be repotted as they outgrow containers.

- Location is important regarding sunlight and heat.

- Good drainage is essential for the health of container plants.

To get started with container gardening, you will need to take the location, containers you will use, and the specific requirements of the herbs you plant into consideration. The location of your containers depends on the space you have available to dedicate to your healing garden.

Some ideas for where to place your container garden include:

- A sunny windowsill
- A back deck or patio
- A front porch
- Entry steps to your home or apartment
- Within an existing outdoor garden
- Window boxes

Herbs planted in containers tend to dry out much faster than those planted directly in the ground as the containers keep soil warmer. For this reason, you will want to locate your container garden where the plants will get shade during the hottest part of the day, but still get sun for at least six hours. Some herbs like mint, parsley and sweet woodruff prefer even less sun and should be located where they can enjoy shade most of the day with only an hour or two of direct sunlight.

When planting several herbs together in one container, it is best to plant herbs together that require similar conditions. *Refer to the tables earlier in this chapter to determine good companion herbs.* When growing herbs in containers, certain herbs like lemon verbena and mint that tend to overcrowd the garden should be grown in individual containers. To determine how much room a plant needs and if it has a tendency to overcrowd other plants, research the growing habits of the particular herb before planting it. A good resource for information on herbs and their specific growing habits in your area is your local Cooperative Extension System office. For a listing of offices by state, visit their website at **http://nifa.usda.gov/partners-and-extension-map**.

When considering which types of containers to use for starting an herb garden, consider proper drainage, personal taste and size. Nearly any type of container can be used for growing herbs as long as it allows proper drainage. For example, terra-cotta planters, decorative dishes, wooden crates, old tires and even shoes can be used depending on personal garden style taste and design. Ensuring that whichever container you choose can properly drain water will be essential to healthy plants. A variety of different planting containers and styles would make for an interesting and whimsical container garden. Paying close attention the size of your container and the growing habit of the herb that is planted in it is also a key factor to the success of healthy plants. A container that is too small will cause the plant to become root bound. A root-bound plant is one whose roots reach the far edges of the container and have nowhere else to grow. This can often cause the plant to grow poorly and even die. A container that is too large will cause root rot because it will hold too much water. Ideally, a container for herb plants should allow for 2 inches of space completely around the plant. Be prepared to repot, if necessary, as the plant grows.

Hanging containers are a great way to display and grow herbs. By pairing culinary herbs together in a hanging basket in a sunny kitchen window, you will have a convenient way to snip a fresh herb or two while cooking. Some herbs that do well in hanging containers include trailing herbs that will spill over the pot and hang down, such as thyme or rosemary. Sage, marjoram and basil also lend themselves to trailing when planting in a hanging basket. Hanging baskets or pots are available at a variety of gardening shops, nurseries and home improvement stores. Most are designed with hooks for hanging directly from a wall or post.

Using containers in your garden allows you the opportunity to ensure good soil for your plants. Using pots or other containers in your garden is a good idea if you live in an area where the soil is poor or polluted. You can purchase container soil mixes from any garden center, local nursery, or home improvement center. Ordinary garden soil will be too heavy for potted herbs and will not drain properly in a container setting. Instead, look for a good high-quality mix that combines soil with lighter materials, like peat moss, and has extra fertilization. Ideally, an organic all-natural fertilizer should be mixed in with the soil prior to potting your plants. In time, your herbs will use all of the nutrients in their container and will need to be re-fertilized. You can do this by adding an organic fertilizer, like fish emulsion, to the soil. Remember to completely repot plants that have outgrown their containers by putting them in a larger pot with new dirt and fertilizer.

With the exception of a few, most medicinal plants will grow well and thrive when grown in containers. Additionally, growing in containers makes moving plants and redesigning the look of a garden an easy task. Herbs with taproots, however, are more difficult to grow well in containers. A **taproot** is a large root structure that goes deep into the ground and has many smaller roots shooting off of the main base. An herb with a taproot can be planted in a very large container to accommodate for its large roots, or planed directly in a garden plot instead.

Properties of Certain Healing Herbs

Examples of Herbs with a Taproot	Examples of Invasive Herbs
Coriander	Herbs in the mint family (peppermint, catmint)
Chicory	Lemon balm
Dill	Thyme
Horseradish	Oregano
Borage	

You can also use containers for very invasive herbs that will take over your garden if they are not contained. For instance, if you plant mints outdoors, you might want to give them a garden plot of their own, or plant them in a container and then bury the container. A container can easily be fully or partially buried to help prevent the herb from spreading throughout the garden. To do so, dig a hole slightly wider than the container you plan to use and as deep as you want to bury it. Then, set the container in the hole, fill with potting soil, and add your herb, or sow the seeds, within the container's walls. Instead of burying the container, you could opt to use it as a decorative accent in your garden.

For a successful container garden:

- Ensure that your container has holes or slits at the bottom to allow proper drainage.
- Use a good potting soil, and fertilize as needed.
- Any container used must be thoroughly cleaned and scrubbed of all dirt to remove any possible contaminants from previous plants that can foster disease.
- Plant herbs together that need the same light, water and soil conditions.
- Ensure plants have enough room to grow, and repot as necessary.
- Do not allow plants to completely dry out.

Raised beds

A raised bed is a planting bed built on top of your soil. This is an easy solution for gardeners with poor soil. Instead of struggling with poor soil conditions, a garden bed is built above ground where you have complete control over soil quality. By starting with bagged soil and adding compost, you can create the ideal growing conditions for your plants. Raised beds, when built to a manageable width, eradicate the problems walking directly in the garden bed can cause. When a garden is walked on, this compacts the soil, limiting the airflow that is essential to good plant growth.

Advantages of raised beds include:

- You can space plants a little closer together than in a conventional garden because you do not need stepping space if you design your beds properly.

- Raised beds will drain excess moisture better than a non-raised bed.

- Soil conditions are more easily controlled in a raised garden bed.

- You can produce more plants per square foot as you do not need to use valuable space for walking paths.

- Raised beds reduce bending and straining because the beds are higher than standard beds that are sowed directly in the ground.

- Raised beds require less maintenance and weed control as the main crops tend to crowd out and discourage weed growth, which leads to less weeding.

Before creating a raised bed, plan ahead. You can make portable raised beds; however, in most cases you will want to build permanent beds. Portable raised beds range from wooden boxes and crates to fiber bags that can be moved easily. Wooden boxes and fiber bags, designed specifically to grow edible plants, are readily available at your local garden center or online. A raised bed should be less than 4 feet wide, unless you add stepping-stones or some sort of path in the center to walk across. By keeping your raised bed no wider than 4 feet, you will be able to easily reach across to plant, weed, and harvest. Raised beds can be any length, depending on the space available in your yard. You can make your own raised beds by stacking stones or bricks. By screwing together untreated, rectangular wooden boards — also known as railway ties — into squares or rectangles, you can also create raised beds. If you prefer to purchase raised beds, you will find them in many shapes, sizes and materials. You can find more information on the various types of raised gardens online or through your local hardware store, nursery, or home improvement store.

When determining the length of the beds, longer is not necessarily better. Two medium-length beds with walking space in between them will make it easier to work with your plants. You can design raised beds so you can tend to your garden from a chair. Raised bed gardens are normally 2½ to 3 feet high, but if you would like to personalize the height, sit in a chair and extend your arms as if you were typing. Measure the distance between the ground and your hands and make your raised beds accordingly. This is a good idea for people who have back problems, are in a wheelchair, or for the elderly who still love to garden.

Plants with similar needs should be placed in the same raised bed. You can divide a bed by adding a wooden plank to separate different kinds of plants or to keep aggressive plants from spreading too much. For example, plants that prefer similar types of soil conditions or pH levels can be grouped together in a single bed. Each raised bed could also have its own theme. Plant a tea garden in one bed with herbs like chamomile, catnip and lemon balm. In another bed, group together primarily culinary herbs that grow well together like garlic and chives.

Creating a raised bed garden will limit the need for maintenance. Each spring or fall, you will simply need to add fresh compost to the beds. *For information on composting, see Chapter 4.* To fully benefit from the added nutrients from the compost, it is important to work the compost into the top 5 to 7 inches of the existing soil. As moisture retention is also important in a raised bed, adding a layer of organic mulch to the top of the soil will not only keep weeds down, but also help lock in moisture. *For information on mulch options, see Chapter 4.* To help ensure your soil drains properly, add an inch or two of stones at the bottom of the bed before adding soil.

Traditional garden

An in-ground field, or traditional garden, should be started three to four months prior to your zone's planting season or during the previous garden season in preparation for the following year. Choose a location that allows for proper sunlight and drainage conditions for the herbal plants. To get started, mark off your garden using stakes and string from corner to corner, or use a garden hose and bend it into a curved garden shape. Clear the area of any large rocks, existing foliage, or debris. If the area has grass, mow the grass close to the ground. Cover the grass with a layer of overlapping newspaper 1 to 3 inches thick to kill the grass. Wet the newspaper by watering thoroughly and cover with 6 to 8 inches of cleaned and screened topsoil or straw and then rewater the newspaper.

You can find various size bags of topsoil at your local garden or home improvement center. The newspaper and subsequent cover will smother the grass and discourage sunlight from fostering new growth. The newspaper will naturally disintegrate into the soil over time. Killing the grass will open up the area to allow you to plant your garden in an area free of other plant matter.

In the spring, when the soil is not frozen and easy to work, add a good fertilizer. Some natural choices include a seaweed or fish mix. Your local garden center will be able to assist you with the options available in your area. This is also an ideal time to work compost into the garden. Compost and fertilizer can be worked into the top of your garden by applying a layer 4 to 6 inches deep and working it in with a tiller or a shovel. Your plot is now ready for planting herbal plants you started indoors or purchased at the nursery, or for starting seeds. Once your herbs are planted, or your seedlings emerge, mulch with your choice of organic mulches. *Refer to Chapter 4 for examples of mulching options.*

Advantages and Disadvantages of Garden Types

Garden Type	Advantages	Disadvantages
Container	Easily moved Offers control over soil Limits pests and weeds Can easily vary garden size	Needs fertilizer Requires more frequent watering Needs to repot as plants grow
Raised beds	Drains moisture well Controls soil conditions Produces higher yields Reduces bending Less weeds Requires less maintenance	Requires building More permanent structure Not easily moved
Traditional garden	Can be any size Plant size does not matter	Requires prep work More maintenance Less soil control More weeds and pests

Design

Regardless of the type of garden you decide to plant, choosing a well-thought-out design is also important. The garden can be beautiful and easy to maintain if planned properly. If you are a novice gardener, start with a few herbs, and increase your garden's size as you feel more comfortable with your gardening skills. Your garden needs to be easily accessible because this will make it easier to maintain the garden and harvest it. When considering design, take into account the possibility of creating a theme for your medicinal herbal garden.

Theme garden

Herbs are very aromatic, easy to grow, and have a multitude of uses. You might want to consider a theme garden or several small theme gardens. For instance, how about an herbal vinegar theme garden? These are great on salads and easy to make at home. Some herbs you can include in this garden would be tarragon, chives, basil, dill, thyme and lemon balm. A garden does not have to contain strictly herbs intended for medicinal use. Adding fresh herbs to food is a very healthy habit, too.

If you enjoy herbal teas, you might consider a tea-themed garden. Herbs can be very fragrant, and a garden of lavender, sage, bergamot, thyme and lemon balm could be grown just for their aromas. The scent of lavender in a garden is especially lovely and calming. You can also cut the herbs and make a bouquet of flowers to use in vases around your home. Aromatic herbs can also be used to make sachets to keep drawers smelling nice or as a natural air freshener. Experiment with combinations of different herbs to discover which scent pairings work best in your home.

Historic herbal gardens are another theme option. Herbs were important during the Middle Ages and were used to mask odors that food spoilage, tooth decay and poor hygiene caused. Pest repellents such as pennyroyal, tansy and wormwood were planted to repel pests from other plants in the garden, as well as from the living areas. Chamomile, lavender and rosemary were traditionally thrown on the floor to mask odors and repel pests; they also made for a great potpourri.

How about a Western hemisphere theme garden? These plants would be native to North and South America. For instance, bee balm, also known as Oswego tea, was given to the colonists by the Oswego Indians to replace the English tea discarded at the Boston Tea Party. Eastern Asia and Pacific herb gardens would include fennel, lemongrass, chives and nutmeg.

Theme garden ideas offer myriad healing garden possibilities from herbs that help with gender-specific health issues to herbs specifically for children. A women's health garden might include angelica for cramping relief and for its high level of iron, chamomile for stress, and motherwort to help balance hormones. A men's health garden might include nettle for strength, St. John's wort for depression, and pumpkin seed for prostate health. A healing herb garden for children might include lavender and chamomile for calming, peppermint for colic, and aloe vera for diaper rash. Perhaps a pet health garden might be beneficial to you. Some herbs to include in a pet health garden might be ginger for pets that get carsick, aloe vera for cuts and dry patches, and oats, lavender, or chamomile for anxiety. Herbs to treat a specific body system could be grouped into a single garden. *Refer to Chapter 9 for information on body systems.* The ideas for theme gardens are endless.

Theme gardens can also be grown in containers and make great gifts. For instance, a medicinal container garden could consist of aloe for burns, dill and peppermint for indigestion, yarrow for cuts, and sage for sore throats.

Formal herb garden

Traditionally, herb gardens were laid out in very formal, geometric designs. This dates back to the Renaissance when gardeners began organizing squares and rectangles into more complex patterns. Most herb gardens were grown by monks who grew herbs primarily for medicinal purposes. They often had symmetrical planting plans, matching herbs on either side of the garden like reflections in a mirror. Even an informal garden looks more pleasing to the eye if the interior spaces are geometric. Interior geometric spaces can be created using pathways and grouping plants of similar heights or colors together. Color groupings and pathway edgings unify a garden in look and design.

Although a formal garden seems intimidating, by choosing a circle or square and dividing it into sections, you can create a simple formal garden. These sections should be of equal size, and you should then fill each section with similar-type plants. Knot gardens, for example, interlace herbs with contrasting foliage color into patterns. A simple knot garden can be made with two overlapping circles or squares on a background of mulch or gravel.

The center of a formal herb garden is often the focal point. For instance, a lovely birdbath centered in your formal garden would complement all the plants used throughout the garden. Formal herb gardens are more labor intensive because you do have to keep the herbs trimmed; however, they are stunning.

A garden sanctuary

A garden is a great place to reflect and take your mind off other concerns and the rigors of daily life. This is a good place to get in touch with nature and yourself. If you have the space, consider adding a garden sanctuary. Select an area in your yard that is somewhat secluded. Making a special entrance into your garden, like a trellis or arch, will create a sense of peace. If you do not have a wall or fence, you can create an enclosure with hedges.

You might want to integrate water into your plan, such as a fountain or a birdbath, because nothing soothes like the sound of water. You can add other elements, such as rocks and wind chimes. Select colors and accessories that have special meaning for you.

You may also want privacy in your garden. Try to create a sense of enclosure with a bench or chair surrounded by lush plants. Choose herbs that attract birds and butterflies, or aromatic herbs such as lavender. Gardening has always been known to be therapeutic. Being in a garden brings peace and relaxation. Imagine working or just sitting in your dream garden while the troubles of life melt away.

Choosing Herbs

Once you decide on the type of garden to grow, it is time to choose the herbs. It is a good idea to make a list of the herbs you will use, along with how tall the herb will grow, its flower color and its spacing requirements. The garden can be organized by coordinated colors, by keeping similar herbs together, or matched by scents. You will need to be able to reach everything in the garden. After deciding the shape and size of the garden plot, sketch it on paper. Looking at your list of herbs, place them in your garden sketch according to height and color. Add the lists and sketches to your planning binder. Remember to note how far apart the plants should be spaced as indicated on the seed packets or tag included in the plant from the garden center. This will be your planting guide.

It is essential to take into consideration each individual plant's spacing requirements when organizing your garden plan because it will grow significantly from the time it is planted in May to its full size in July. There are some herbs that grow in clumps and need to be spaced a good distance from each other, while others do not need a large space between plants. Paying attention and planning for each individual plant's growing requirements and size will positively impact the look and health of your garden.

The hardiness of each plant will determine when the herb can be planted in your garden. Most plants are usually planted in spring. By reading the seed packets or instructions that come with the plants, you will be able to determine their ideal planting time. Most plants require a planting time that is when all danger of frost has passed. To figure out the frost date in your growing location, consult an extension office, a local garden center, or an almanac for the approximate frost dates for your area.

In addition to proper temperature and space requirements, the height and color of the herbs will also need to be taken into consideration. Tall herb plants, for example, should be placed at the back of the garden as not to block out the sun or hide smaller plants. The information about a specific plant's height can be found on the back of the seed packet or the information tag on the plant. Varying plant height and color in an herb garden will greatly add to its visual appeal. Color is a significant element in composing an aesthetically pleasing herb garden. Most herbs will complement each other in the garden. However, if too many plants of the same color are grouped together, the effect might be overwhelming and the individual plant will go unnoticed. Color variation occurs in the bloom and foliage of the plant. By breaking up similar colored plants with ones of another shade, for example, the eye will roam from one plant to another. Contrary to the popular belief that all shades of plant "greens" are the same, herb foliage can range in color from silvery grey to yellow green to a deep bluish green.

Examples of Healing Herb "Green" Foliage Variations

Grey-Green	Yellow-Green	Blue-Green	Other Colors
Borage	Feverfew	Chives	Basil, *opal*
Catnip	Lemon balm	Hyssop	(brownish-purple)
Lavender	Mint, *pineapple*		Comfrey, variegated
Sage	Sage, *golden*		Fennel, *bronze*
Thyme, *tiny leaf*	Thyme, *lemon*		Sage, *purple*

While planning a garden, you will become more familiar with each plant and its needs. Once you determine the type of garden you want to create and establish its location, choosing the herbs to include in it will be the next step. The next chapter is a list of useful healing herbs with details on different characteristics to help in the selection process.

Chapter 3

USEFUL HEALING HERBS

Learning about specific herbs, their properties and planting requirements will help you make informed decisions about which plants you may want to include in your healing herb garden. As you make your plant selections, pay particular attention to their growing zones, sun and soil conditions, and medicinal uses. This chapter will provide a description of each herb, the best time to plant, sun and soil requirements, when to harvest, parts of the plant used, propagation methods, and medicinal uses. Although not a complete list of all medicinal herbs, this chapter is a good resource to learn about a variety of healing plants available to the home gardener.

Aloe

Aloe barbadensis

Description

Aloe is a succulent, which is a plant accustomed to arid conditions with fleshy leaves that store water — cactus is also a succulent. Known as the "medicine plant," aloe is often used externally to treat burns and other skin ailments. This is a perennial that can grow 2 to 3 feet tall. This plant grows outdoors in zones 9 and 10, but is often grown indoors because it is very useful and decorative. The leaves are fleshy and sword-shaped with spiny edges. Keep one on the windowsill in the kitchen in the event of a minor burn or cut.

When to plant

Container-grown aloe plants can be planted in the garden anytime; just remember to bring them indoors during winter. Aloe can be planted directly in the ground at any time; however, unless you live in an arid climate, it should be brought in during the cold winter months.

Sun and soil

Aloe prefers full sun, but can tolerate partial shade. Plant it in well-drained soil and allow 1 to 2 feet between plants if you are growing it outdoors. Aloe does not require constant watering. It also has a tendency to develop root rot if its soil is continually wet. Aloe should be watered only when the top inch of soil is dry.

When to harvest

Cut a leaf off any time it is needed, cutting the oldest, larger leaves first.

Parts used

The leaves of the aloe plant are used for medicinal purposes.

Propagation

Aloe forms offshoots, or new plant growth, near the base of the plant. Remove the plant gently from the pot and carefully pull any offshoots away from the mother plant. The offshoots will create roots of their own once planted in the soil.

Medicinal benefits

Aloe is well known in a variety of cultures around the world for healing skin injuries. Split the leaf and rub the gel inside the leaf on a burn, scald, sunburn or cut. The aloe gel will dry and form a film over the wound like a natural bandage.

Angelica
Angelica archangelica

Description

Angelica is a biennial that can grow up to 8 feet tall and grows best in zones 4 to 9. The leaves are broad with toothed edges and can grow 2 feet long. Its flowers are similar to Queen Anne's lace and can be up to 10 inches in diameter. This plant's small, green flowers smell like honey. The plants bloom in June or July in the second year of growth. The plants die back in the winter months and will return from the same roots the following spring. There is a mild licorice flavor to the plant parts that can be used to help fight colds, fevers and minor aches.

When to plant

Angelica is difficult to transplant, so starting from seeds is the best method. Gather seeds in late summer or early fall and sow them. If you purchase angelica seeds, refrigerate them until it is time to plant.

Sun and soil

Angelica will grow in the sun if it is in a mulched area to keep its roots cool and moist, but prefers partial shade. The soil should be moderately moist and slightly acidic. Ideally, angelica should be spaced 5 feet apart to allow for its larger size.

When to harvest

Harvest this plant in spring and summer, but before the plants flower. Many of the nutrients in the plant go to the flower, and in this case, the flower is not used for healing, which is why it is important to harvest before the flower is produced. Gather leaves and stems during the spring and summer in the morning after the dew is dried. Seeds are collected in late summer when they are nearly ripe, and you can preserve them by enclosing the entire seed head in a paper bag and shaking gently. The roots can be dug up in early fall after one year and dried or used fresh. Cut the stems where the leaf attaches, and strip the leaves from the stems. Angelica dies after seeding, so if you do not want the seeds, cut the flowers off early to prolong the life of the plant. Hang leaves and enclosed seed heads to dry. The stems can be cut into 2-inch pieces to dry in a dehydrator or on a screen outdoors.

Parts used

The roots, leaves and seeds are used for medicinal purposes.

Medicinal benefits

Angelica is known to enhance circulation and is also used as a mild expectorant to facilitate the expulsion of phlegm and mucus. Angelica relaxes the windpipe and may be beneficial in treating bronchitis and asthma. It may also increase the blood's ability to clot. Angelica can be used in an infusion, decoction or tincture. *See Chapter 8 for details on ways in which to use herbs.* Angelica should not be given to children under the age of 2.

Astragalus

Astragalus membranaceus

Description

Astragalus, also known as huang qi, is a perennial that grows best in zones 6 through 11. It grows to 3 or 4 feet tall and has pale yellow, pea-shaped flowers that grow from midsummer through the frost season.

When to plant

To start astragalus from seed, stratify seeds for three weeks by refrigerating them. Then, scarify them by roughing up the outer shell of seeds with sandpaper or by puncturing so water can enter, and soak in warm water for an hour before planting. Start seeds indoors and transplant outside after last frost. Sow outdoors in early spring, and plant them about 15 inches apart.

Sun and soil

Astragalus prefers sun to partial shade and dry, sandy soil. Water moderately.

When to harvest

Roots should be harvested after the plants are at least 2 years old.

Parts used

Roots, either fresh or dried, are used.

Medicinal benefits

Astragalus is used in traditional Chinese herbal medicine and is known for its strong immune system support. Some people use astragalus in soup when they have a cold or the flu. It is most often used as a tonic, tincture, decoction, or syrup.

Basil, Sweet

Ocimum basilicum

Description

Basil is an annual that grows 1 to 2 feet tall with small white, pink, or purple flowers that bloom from midsummer to fall. Common basil has glossy, deep green leaves with smooth edges, although the "ruffles" variety has frilled leaves with toothed edges. Basil is a tender annual in most zones and grows best outdoors during the hot summer months. Additionally, basil can be grown indoors on a sunny windowsill.

When to plant

Basil is easily grown from seed, and germination usually takes about a week. You can start the plant indoors six weeks before the last frost and transplant it after all danger of frost passes. Space the plants 12 to 18 inches apart. Sow seeds directly outdoors once all danger of frost has passed.

Sun and soil

Basil needs well-drained, moist soil and mulching. It prefers full sun, but will grow in partial shade.

When to harvest

Cut leaves and stems when plants are 8 inches tall and before they bloom. Basil can be harvested at any time throughout the growing season. Cut or pinch off branch tips, always leaving at least one pair of leaves below the cut so that new branches can form. Basil stems can be cut and kept in a jar of water in your kitchen for several days, making them handy to use in cooking. You can hang the basil upside down to dry, or it can be frozen in ice cube trays with olive oil after plunging the basil into boiling water for just a couple of minutes, which is a process is called **blanching**.

Parts used

The leaves, either fresh or dried, are used in medicine.

Medicinal benefits

Use as an infusion to promote digestion. Use an infusion or tincture to fight infections.

Bee Balm

Monarda didyma, red or purple
Monarda fistulosa, pink

Description

Bee balm, also commonly called bergamot, is a perennial herb native to the eastern part of North America. It grows naturally from Ontario to Mexico. Bee balm was used as a medicinal plant by the Native Americans.

Characterized by showy red, purple, or pink flowers, bee balm stands about 3 feet tall. The square-shaped stem of bee balm supports light green leaves that occur in opposite pairs on each side of the stem.

When to plant

Bee balm is easiest to start when purchased as a plant from your local garden center. It can be planted in spring and will spread rapidly throughout your garden during the growing season. It can also be sown directly into the garden in spring. Bee balm grows best in zones 3 through 9. Space the plants 8 to 12 inches apart for maximum growth potential.

Sun and soil

Bee balm can grow in a variety of soil conditions from ordinary garden soil to clay. It prefers partial shade to sun, and it will really flourish in a dry, alkaline soil.

When to harvest

The flowers from the bee balm plant should be harvested in June or July for peak flavor and fragrance. The stems and leaves can be harvested throughout the growing season.

Parts used

The flowers, leaves and stems of the bee balm plant are used for medicinal purposes.

Medicinal benefits

Bee balm is used as a garnish in salads, adds a lemony scent to potpourri and is also used in many medicinal treatments. The leaves, flowers and stems can be used as an antiseptic and diuretic. An infusion of bee balm can be used internally to treat colds, headaches, sore throats, menstrual cramps, nausea, fever and gastric complaints. Boiling bee balm in a pan and inhaling the steam can help with bronchial inflammation.

Black-eyed Susan

Rudbeckia hirta

Description

Native to North America, the black-eyed Susan is the official state flower of Maryland. *Rudbeckia hirta* is a yellow, daisy-like flower with a dark brown center. It was named by the botanist Carolus Linneaus to honor the Swedish physician and royally revered botanist Olaus Olai Rudbeck (1660-1740). The plant ranges in height from 18 to 72 inches and is available in a variety of shades of gold and yellow. They bloom late summer to fall and are hardy in zones 3 to 7.

When to plant

Black-eyed Susan can be planted in spring by seed or plant division. To divide black-eyed Susan, gently dig up the entire plant and separate it into several smaller plants by pulling it apart at the root. The seeds, however, need to be stratified to recreate the natural cold and thaw cycle. You can do this by placing them in a zip-top bag for four weeks in the freezer. Another option is to sow them in the ground during the fall and let winter naturally do the stratification work for you. If planting by seed directly outdoors, the plants will need to be thinned to a spacing of 12 inches between each plant.

Sun and soil

Black-eyed Susans prefer full sun and can thrive in almost any soil condition. Soil with too much nitrogen, however, may kill the plant. To find out if your soil has too much nitrogen, you may want to test it before planting black-eyed Susans.

When to harvest

The roots of the plant should be dug up in either spring or fall and not during the plant's peak summer growing season. Leaves can be gathered throughout the growing season.

Parts used

The leaves and roots of the black-eyed Susan plant are used for medicinal purposes.

Medicinal benefits

Black-eyed Susan is used to support heart health, women's health concerns like cramping, and as a diuretic. This herb can be used as an infusion or tincture.

Boneset

Eupatorium perfoliatum

Description

A perennial native to the eastern United States, boneset belongs to the same botanical family as echinacea. It has loose, flat-topped white flowers, deep green leaves and hairy stems. This is a low-maintenance plant that is great for attracting butterflies. It grows to a height of 3 to 4 feet and grows best in zones 4 to 8.

When to plant

Boneset is easy to start from seed or cuttings and may be transplanted in early spring. Cuttings can be taken throughout the growing season and rooted directly into the soil to create new plants. You can also cut it back in early spring and fertilize to promote bushiness for a healthier and higher-yield producing plant. Start with root divisions planted in spring or fall.

Sun and soil

This plant will grow in sandy to clay soils, but needs constant moisture. It likes partial shade to full sun and should be spaced 24 to 30 inches apart.

When to harvest

Harvest boneset throughout the growing season while it is in bloom by cutting the entire plant and hanging it upside down to dry.

Parts used

The leaves and flowering tops are used in medicinal remedies.

Medicinal benefits

This herb can be used as a tea or tincture to remedy fever-related conditions, cold, sore throat, or flu.

Borage

Borago officinalis

Description

Borage is an annual that can grow up to 3 feet tall, but usually grows to about 1 to 2 feet. It has blue, star-shaped flowers with black anthers, which is the part of the flower that holds the pollen on top of the stamen. It has broad, hairy leaves with prominent veins. The branches can grow out about 3 feet, making a lovely round shape. Bees love to pollinate this plant. It grows well with strawberries, and is thought to keep pesky insects off surrounding plants.

When to plant

Start indoors six to eight weeks before the last frost, preferably in peat or newspaper pots. Newspaper pots are pots you can make yourself from newspaper that will decompose in the soil when planted. Transplant seedlings to the garden or sow directly in the garden after all danger of frost passes. Allow about 2 feet on all sides of the plant to allow for growth. It will self-seed easily, reducing the need to replant the following season.

Sun and soil

Borage prefers moist, well-drained soil and likes full sun in cooler climates, but will tolerate partial shade in southern regions of the country. Borage is highly susceptible to root rot if the soil is too soggy.

When to harvest

Leaves can be harvested anytime during the growing season, and flowers can be picked when they are fully open. Harvest the plant after dew has dried. You can strip stems off leaves or pick individual leaves. Snip each flower or the entire cluster.

Parts used

The leaves and flowers are used in healing remedies.

Medicinal benefits

Borage tea is used as a strengthening tonic for patients with fatigue, depression, or arthritis. It is also used to break fevers and detoxify the system. It has a diuretic action to help rid the body of toxins through the skin by promoting sweating and is used to help clear up eruptions of the skin, such as acne, boils and rashes. The mucilage in borage also helps clear chest congestion. It stimulates the adrenal glands to produce hormones the body needs to function properly. It is especially useful during menopause.

Calendula

Calendula officinalis

Description

This annual, also called the Scotch marigold, grows to about 18 inches tall with bright yellow or orange flowers that are sometimes used to add color to salads. Calendula blooms from early summer to the time of the first frost, and its leaves are oval with smooth edges.

When to plant

Calendula is easy to start from seed, and germination takes about one to two weeks. Plant directly into soil after all danger of frost passes. This plant grows in clumps, so space about 10 inches apart.

Sun and soil

This herb prefers full sun, except in the most intense heat. It grows well in most soils.

When to harvest

Pick flowers when fully opened, but before they start to form seeds. When the flowers start to seed, they are not medicinally active. Remove dead blossoms and separate petals to dry. By removing dead blossoms, it will also promote blooming of additional flowers.

Parts used

The flowers, either fresh or dried, are the parts used for medicinal reasons.

Medicinal benefits

An infusion of calendula is good for washing infected skin to prevent staph infection. Apply topically for sunburn or diaper rash. Calendula can also be taken internally as a tea or tincture for gastritis.

California Poppy

Eschscholzia californica

Description

Used for thousands of years by the Pima and Yokut Indians, the California poppy is native to the west coast of North America. A close relative of the opium poppy, the California poppy is primarily used for its calming effects. Considered an annual in cooler zones, it grows about 2 feet tall. The flowers are bright orange with four, 2-inch long petals that balance on tall, thin stalks.

When to plant

Plant seeds directly in the garden during late spring. The seeds need to be stratified for a week prior to planting. The California poppy tends to self-sow, and you could end up with a decent-size patch from year to year. The plants should be spaced 10 to 12 inches apart.

Sun and soil

This herb is drought-tolerant and prefers sun to partial shade. California poppy prefers to grow in poor, not well-fertilized soils.

When to harvest

You can harvest the entire plant when it is in full bloom for both the poppy flower and seedpods.

Parts used

The whole plant, fresh or dried, is used for healing purposes.

Medicinal benefits

This herb can be used for pain relief, as a sleep aid, and to reduce stress and anxiety. The California poppy can be used in a variety of ways including as a syrup, infused oil, salve, cream, infusion, tincture, compress, foot soak,and elixir.

Caution

A warning about poppy seed consumption: Poppy seeds are also a source of opium, from which heroin and other narcotics are derived. Because of this, poppy seeds may create a positive result in drug testing.

Catnip

Nepeta cataria

Description

Cats love this herb. It is interesting to note that it acts as a stimulant for cats and a sedative for people. Catnip is a perennial that grows to about 2 feet tall. It has spikes of pinkish/purple or white flowers that bloom through the summer. Its leaves are heart-shaped with toothed margins, and its stems and leaves are covered with soft hairs. It dies back in the winter months.

When to plant

Sow directly outdoors in mid-spring, and place the plants 8 inches apart. This plant can be started indoors and then transplanted outside. Germination is better if seeds are stratified for about three weeks prior to planting. You might want to put a cage around this plant to keep the cats out until it is well established.

Sun and soil

Catnip really has no special soil needs, but it does like moist, well-drained soil. In the North, it prefers full sun and in the South, partial shade.

When to harvest

Wait for the plant to bloom and then harvest the leaves in the morning after the dew dries. You can snip off the individual leaves, but if harvesting to dry, cut the entire plant at the stem about 2 inches above the ground and hang upside down to air-dry.

Parts used

The flowers and leaves, either fresh or dried, are used.

Medicinal benefits

A cup of catnip tea aids digestion after dinner. Catnip is also good to take before bed to induce sleep, and it can be used in a sleep pillow. It can be used as a tea, tincture, infusion, or decoction. Weak infusions can be given to colicky infants.

Cayenne

Capsicum minimum

Description

Cayenne is an annual that grows to about 2 feet tall. It develops small white blooms prior to the development of the green chilies, which turn bright red when ripe. Cayenne can be grown in zones 7 through 11.

When to plant

Start cayenne indoors in early spring in a sunny location, and the seeds will germinate in about a week. Transplant the herb outdoors, spaced about 12 inches apart, after all danger of frost passes.

Sun and soil

Cayenne prefers full sun and requires little watering. Additionally, cayenne has no specific soil requirements.

When to harvest

Pick the chilies when they turn red, which usually happens in late summer and early fall. It is recommended to use gloves, as the capsicum resin on the skin of the chilies can burn human skin.

Parts used

Only the chilies are used for healing purposes. Never eat the leaves, stems, or flowers, as they can be toxic.

Medicinal benefits

Cayenne is very beneficial for the heart and circulatory health. The capsaicin in cayenne is the active ingredient in many arthritis creams and can help relieve pain in joints and muscles because it desensitizes nerve endings. Add dried cayenne to mix into a liniment, a topical medical ointment. Some people use the tincture with tomato juice for a heart-health daily drink.

Caution

Do not get cayenne in the eyes.

Celery

Apium graveolens

Description

Celery is a sometimes difficult plant to grow that originated in the wet plains of the Mediterranean basin. Although primarily considered a vegetable today, celery was originally used as a medicinal plant. The oils and seeds of the celery plant have been used since ancient times to treat colds, the flu and digestive issues. Celery is hardy in zones 5 and warmer.

When to plant

Celery needs a long time to germinate and has a long growing season. Therefore, you should start celery indoors by seed sometime in March. Prior to planting, the seeds need to be stratified for several weeks in the freezer and then soaked overnight. Celery takes 120 to 140 days to reach maturity.

Sun and soil

Celery is vulnerable to dry weather, does not like the cold and is picky about its soil conditions. It should be planted in full sun and heavily composted soil. Space celery plants 12 inches apart. Celery needs to be frequently watered and should not be allowed to dry out.

When to harvest

Harvest this plant when the stalks are fully grown and have reached about 1 foot tall.

Parts used

The stalks and leaves of the celery plant can be used for medicinal purposes.

Medicinal benefits

Celery provides many health benefits. It can lower blood pressure, improve circulation, help with cold and flu resistance, and even inhibit cancer development. Studies reported by the *Proceeding of the National Academy of Science* indicate that the nutrient luteolin found in celery helps protect against DNA mutations that damage cells and cause cancer.

Chamomile

Marticaria recutita and *Chamaemelum nobile*

Description

German chamomile and Roman chamomile have white flowers that look like daisies with yellow centers. Roman chamomile has long stems that creep along the ground away from the main plant and coarse leaves. German chamomile, on the other hand, is more erect with feathery leaves.

When to plant

Sow outdoors when soil is about 55 to 60 degrees through the night. German chamomile is the most common form of chamomile found in the United States. Sow the tiny seeds in well-prepared soil, gently pat them down and keep moist.

Sun and soil

This herb prefers a well-drained, sandy soil, and grows in full sun and partial shade. Chamomile is hardy in zones 4 through 9.

When to harvest

When flowers are in full bloom, pinch them off or cut the whole stem. With the whole stem, the flowers can be dried upside down. If you do not cut the stem, dry flowers only on tightly woven drying screens.

Parts used

The flowers and flowering tops can be used from the chamomile plant, either fresh or dried.

Medicinal benefits

Most everyone loves the soothing quality of chamomile tea, and the tea made from your own homegrown chamomile is even better. The tea is sleep-inducing and can also be used as a digestive herb. Weak infusions can be given to small children to aid in digestion, calmness and to help induce sleep.

Chicory

Cichorium intybus

Description

Chicory is most well known for its use as an additive to coffee to enhance flavor. Chicory grows as a wild roadside plant and is native to North America, Australia and Europe. With periwinkle-colored flowers, chicory is a hardy perennial in zones 3 through 10.

When to plant

Chicory can be planted by seed either indoors or directly outdoors in the garden. For ideal germination, stratify seeds before planting. Plant these seeds outdoors mid to late spring about 10 inches apart.

Sun and soil

Preferring to grow wild, the chicory plant has no specific soil requirements. It does, however, prefer full sun.

When to harvest

The roots of the chicory plant should be harvested in either the spring or fall. Its leaves can be picked throughout the growing season. Flowers of the chicory plant can be harvested throughout the growing season as well.

Parts used

The leaves, roots, and flowers from this plant are used. The chicory root can be ground and added to coffee to enhance flavor and provide medicinal benefits. When roasted and brewed, chicory has a taste similar to coffee but does not contain caffeine. Parts of the chicory plant can also be used in a tincture, as a syrup, or added to a meal as food.

Medicinal benefits

Chicory is used to support urinary tract health and can also benefit the digestive system. It is also a diuretic, a laxative, and can assist the liver and gallbladder in properly functioning by removing excess water and toxins from these vital organs. Chicory is rich in vitamin A and can help support eye health.

Chives

Allium Schoenoprasum

Description

Belonging to the plant family that includes onion, garlic, shallot and leek, chives are a hardy perennial across most of the northern hemisphere. Their usage dates back to China in 3,000 B.C. Chives are characterized by long, hollow green stalks that can grow up to 2 feet long. Attractive round lavender flowers bloom on the tops of the long chive stalks.

When to plant

Plant or divide in early spring or fall. Chives can be started by seed or crown division and should be spaced 6 to 9 inches apart. Chives are hardy in zones 3 through 10.

Sun and soil

Chives can tolerate a variety of soils, but prefer full to partial sun to thrive.

When to harvest

Chives can be harvested when the stalks turn green and are several inches out of the ground. Harvesting prior to flowering will enhance the flavor and fragrance of the herb. When harvesting, cut the plant down to about 2 inches from the ground to promote the growth of another crop during the season.

Parts used

Chive flowers can be added to salads, and the stems can be used in a variety of cooking applications to add flavor and decoration.

Medicinal benefits

Because chives have mild anti-inflammatory properties, they can aid in the fight against cancers to reduce inflammation of the tissues. The National Cancer Institute lists several studies that have shown a correlation between increased intake of plants in the allium family and reduced risk of certain cancers. The cancers studied include those of the stomach, colon, esophagus, pancreas and breast. Ancient Romans used chives to cure sore throats and relieve sunburn.

Chrysanthemum

Leucanthemum maximum

Description

Commonly referred to as mums, chrysanthemum comes from the Greek word meaning "golden flower." There are many varieties of this plant, and the flowers come in many shapes and colors including golden yellow, white, reddish, purple-brown and orange. Chrysanthemums were originally grown in Europe and Asia.

When to plant

Plant seeds in the early spring after all danger of frost passes. Mums can also be started from cuttings or divisions and are very easy to grow. When dividing and planting, dig the hole extra deep, as this plant does not like its roots to stay wet. Space plants 18 inches apart. They will usually be among the last flowers alive in your garden, living longer than other plants. Chrysanthemums also grow well in containers.

Sun and soil

Chrysanthemums should be planted in fertile, well-draining, sandy soil and grow best in full sun in zones 3 through 9.

When to harvest

Pick flowers when in full bloom and dry on a screen or in a dehydrator.

Parts used

The flower heads are the only part that is used.

Medicinal benefits

The chrysanthemum is a very important Chinese herb that is used as a tea for headaches and dizziness. Chinese herbal medicine also teaches that chrysanthemum corrects imbalances in the liver and kidneys that cause blurred vision, dry or red eyes, dizziness, and spots in front of the eyes.

Cilantro / Coriander

Coriandrum sativum

Description

Grown around the world for its culinary properties, the leaves of this medicinal plant are given the name cilantro, while the seeds are referred to as coriander. Cilantro and coriander have been used in cooking since prior to 5,000 B.C. and are mentioned in Sanskrit texts and the Bible.

The leaves and stems have a distinctive, strong odor, and the plant will grow 10 to 12 inches in height. The entire plant is edible and will grow in moist gardens in tropical and temperate climates. It is considered an annual and will not tolerate extremely hot conditions.

When to plant

Coriander seeds will not sow well under hot conditions. Sow the seeds outdoors in mid-spring or even in late summer or early fall. The plants need to be spaced 8 to 10 inches apart for optimal growing.

Sun and soil

Cilantro has no specialized soil requirements and will tolerate full sun, shade, or partial shade.

When to harvest

Harvest leaves and stems prior to flowering for maximum taste, oil and fragrance. Seeds can be picked by hand once the plant has fully gone to seed.

Parts used

Leaves, stems and seeds are used. In addition to adding it as a flavoring to foods, it can be made into cider vinegar tinctures.

Medicinal benefits

Cilantro/coriander is very good for digestive health and is considered an appetite stimulant. It is also rich in vitamin C, and the oils found in the leaves of the cilantro plant contain antibacterial properties.

Cinnamon

Cinnamomum Schaeff

Description

One of the oldest known spices, cinnamon comes from a tree that grows up to 50 feet in the wild and is native to Sri Lanka, Brazil, India, Egypt and Vietnam. It has been used medicinally, as flavoring to foods, and as an embalming agent. The bark of the cinnamon tree is dried and rolled into sticks for use.

When to plant

Cinnamon can only be grown and cultivated in tropical climates. The cinnamon tree can be planted at any time. In the United States, it will only grow in zones 9 through 11. In the wild, it reaches 50 feet, but it can reach only about 10 feet tall when cultivated.

Sun and soil

Cinnamon prefers a moist soil in a tropical climate. It will need full sun to grow properly.

When to harvest

The tree must be grown for two years before harvesting its bark for use, as the bark will peel away more easily. The bark should be harvested during the rainy season to make it easier to work with.

Parts used

Bark is ground or scraped off the tree and rolled into sticks.

Medicinal benefits

Cinnamon has been used in traditional Chinese medicine for indigestion, diabetes treatment and colds. It can also be used to help control body odor as part of a natural deodorant and for weight loss. Cinnamon can also calm nausea.

Comfrey

Symphytum officinale

Description

Comfrey is a perennial that grows 3 to 5 feet tall. This herb grows best in zones 3 through 9. It has drooping, bell-shaped flowers that range from yellow to cream and even blue. Comfrey has large, hairy, oval leaves with smooth edges.

When to plant

In the North, plant root divisions in early spring; in the South, plant this herb in the early fall. Comfrey plants need to be spaced a minimum of 3 feet apart because they can grow up to 3 feet wide.

Sun and soil

Comfrey prefers full sun, but will tolerate partial shade. It likes a moist soil.

When to harvest

Pick young leaves during the spring and early summer. It is always best to gather in the morning after the dew dries. The roots are harvested in the fall after the plant begins to die. Dig up the roots and harvest only the smaller rhizomes, or little roots, growing from the side of the central root. Replant the central root.

Parts used

You can use the leaves and roots, either fresh or dried. Dry the roots by cutting them into 1-inch pieces and placing them on a screen to air dry or putting them into a dehydrator.

Medicinal benefits

Comfrey is used externally and contains allatoin, which accelerates tissue healing and helps close wounds. It is a popular addition to herbal salves. Used as a tincture or infusion, it promotes healing of wounds, burns and bruises. Make a decoction of comfrey root to stop bleeding of a minor cut by boiling the root in water for ten to 15 minutes.

Corn

Zea mays

Description

Commonly grown to harvest the kernel-laden vegetable, corn can also be grown medicinally for the silk that sprouts out of the top of the corn ears. Corn is an annual that grows in straight, tall stalks that produce ears of cobs with kernels that are in a protective husk and tufted with silks.

When to plant

Corn is planted by seed directly in the garden after all danger of frost passes. It needs to be spaced in rows 2 to 3 feet apart to ensure proper pollination from one plant to another.

Sun and soil

Corn prefers full sun to partial shade and needs well-drained, nutrient-rich soil to prosper.

When to harvest

Corn should be harvested just as the silks turn brown and the ears are plump and rounded.

Parts used

The corn silk of the plant is used for medicinal purposes and the vegetable is used for food.

Medicinal benefits

Corn silk can be used to relieve water retention caused by kidney disease, PMS, cystitis, and urinary and prostate infections. It can also be used as a tincture to aid in bed-wetting problems in children, as it soothes bladder irritation and reduces frequent urination.

Dandelion

Taraxacum officinale

Description

Dandelion is a perennial that grows to about 8 inches tall with bright, yellow flowers. This plant is often thought of as a weed and self-seeds vigorously, although it has excellent medicinal qualities. If you live in a city, you will want to be sure to remove the flowers before they go to seed and blow into your neighbor's yard.

When to plant

Dandelion seeds germinate quickly, indoors or out. They grow in clumps, so space plants 10 to 12 inches apart. Plant the herbs outdoors in mid- to late spring.

Sun and soil

Dandelion will grow just about anywhere, in full sun or partial sun. It does not have any special soil requirements.

When to harvest

The whole plant is harvested any time during growing. The flowers alone are picked from spring through the fall.

Parts used

All parts of the dandelion are used for medicinal purposes.

Medicinal benefits

Dandelion works well as a whole body tonic and works in nearly every body system, including circulatory, digestive, immune, muscular, reproductive and respiratory. It is particularly beneficial to the liver, urinary tract and skin. The leaves are a diuretic and the roots are a blood purifier. The plant is used as an infusion, decoction and tincture.

Dill

Anethum graveolens

Description

Dill is an annual that grows 3 to 5 feet tall and is native to Eastern Europe and Western Asia. Dill features feathery leaves on a hollow stem. It bears a significant number of yellow flowers when it blooms in mid- to late summer. The word dill comes from the old Norse word "dilla," which means "to lull," as it was often used to lull a colicky child's stomach discomforts.

When to plant

Dill can easily be grown from seed sown directly in the garden after all danger of frost passes. Dill plants should be spaced 12 to 15 inches apart.

Sun and soil

Dill needs to be planted in well-draining soil and in full sun.

When to harvest

The leaves and seeds can be harvested from mid-July through late August for their maximum potential.

Parts used

The leaves and seeds are often used from the dill plant.

Medicinal benefits

Although primarily used for its culinary purposes, dill can also be used as an infusion, syrup, or elixir to assist in settling digestive discomforts.

Echinacea

Echinacea angustifolia and *Echinacea purpurea*

Description

Known as the purple coneflower, *echinacea purpurea* is a perennial that grows best in zones 3 through 9. It has pinkish-purple flowers that bloom in the summer, and it grows 2 to 3 feet tall. *Echinacea angustfolia* has a white flower, but otherwise its characteristics are the same as *E. purpurea.*

When to plant

The seeds should be stratified for about three months before planting. You can start the plant indoors and transplant the seeds in the late spring. Seeds can take from two to six weeks to sprout. They grow in clumps, so space them 12 inches apart.

Sun and soil

E. purpurea requires more water than *E. angustifolia,* and both like full sun. Water the plant regularly, but do not keep it too moist.

When to harvest

Roots are not harvested until they are about 3 years old. *E. angustifolia* has roots that are easier to harvest because they are thinner. The entire plant can be harvested from the second growing season onward. Harvest the whole plant when the flowers are in full bloom.

Parts used

The whole plant, either fresh or dried, should be used.

Medicinal benefits

This plant is well-known as the herb of choice for colds, flu, immune support and respiratory ailments. Use in an infusion, decoction, tincture or salve.

Elder

Sambucus nigra

Description

Elder is a well-known healing plant that was used during the time of Hippocrates and during the Middle Ages. The flowers, bark and berries have been used throughout the centuries to aid in a variety of ailments. Elder bushes are a hardy plant that will grow in a variety of climates and can often be found growing wild along roadsides. The elder bush produces elderberries that are small and dark and grow in clusters.

When to plant

Hardy in zones 4 through 9, plant this herb 6 to 10 inches apart in spring. Keep new plants well watered when first planted as they have a shallow root system. Elder can be propagated from hardwood cuttings in the fall.

Sun and soil

Elder grows best in well-drained, fertile, moist soil and prefers sun to partial shade.

When to harvest

The fruit of the elder should be harvested late July through August. Uncooked berries will be dark purple and inedible. You need to cook the berries prior to eating them as they are poisonous in their natural form.

Parts used

Elderberries and flowers are the only parts used. The white flowers can be used in tonics, brewed into wines, battered and fried, or added to muffins and cakes. Once cooked, the ripe berries can be made into syrups, jams, or even dyes. Cooking will not remove the flower's medicinal qualities.

Medicinal benefits

Elderberries are an effective flu-fighting fruit. They are also good for allergies, fever, sinus issues, reducing the swelling of bruises, coughs, colds, inflammation and pain in the bowels.

Caution

Do not use the leaves, stems, twigs, or roots from the elder tree as they can be poisonous. The berries should always be cooked prior to using to ensure full removal of any toxins.

Elecampane

Inula helenium

Description

This is a tall perennial that grows best in zones 4 through 9. It has yellow daisy-like flowers and will grow to a height of 4 to 6 feet, and it is often seen in the wild near streams and ponds.

When to plant

Seeds should be stratified in a zip-top bag in the refrigerator or freezer for five to seven weeks prior to being started indoors and transplanted in the late spring. They can also be sown directly outdoors in mid-spring. Germination takes about two weeks. Space plants 3 feet apart.

Sun and soil

Elecampane likes rich, **loamy soil** — a combination of sand, clay, silt and organic matter — and full sun to partial shade. It needs moderate amounts of water.

When to harvest

Harvest the roots in the spring or fall.

Parts used

The roots, either fresh or dried, are used.

Medicinal benefits

This herb is very good for the respiratory tract and winter illnesses. It is most often used in a decoction or tincture.

Fennel

Foeniculum vulgare

Description

Fennel is a perennial grown as an annual in most parts of the country. It grows to a height of 4 to 5 feet with flat-topped round yellow flowers, known as umbels, which bloom until frost. The leaves are a feathery blue/green. Fennel is hardy in zones 4 through 10.

When to plant

Fennel is easily grown from seed one to two weeks before the last frost, and it sprouts in about two weeks. Because it grows in clumps, it should be spaced about 12 inches apart.

Sun and soil

Fennel likes full sun and well-drained soil that is moderately fertile with a variety of available nutrients. Do not overwater, as this plant is prone to root rot.

When to harvest

Harvest the roots in spring or fall. Leaves can be handpicked any time. The seeds can be harvested when still green or fully ripened.

Parts used

Seeds, leaves and roots are all used, either fresh or dried.

Medicinal benefits

Fennel promotes milk production in nursing mothers. It is also good for the respiratory tract and the throat. It is an excellent herbal tea for infants with gas or colic. Use it as an infusion, tincture, syrup, compress, or as food.

Feverfew

Chrysanthemum parthenium

Description

Feverfew is a perennial that grows to a height of 2 feet. It grows best in zones 4 through 9, but will grow in most temperate climates. It has small, white daisy-like flowers with yellow centers that usually bloom from midsummer to the end of the season. It has light green leaves that are divided into three segments. The top of the plant dies during winter and regrows from the same roots in the spring.

When to plant

Sow indoors about eight weeks before the last frost, and transplant after all danger of frost passes, or sow outdoors in mid-spring. Space the seeds about 12 inches apart. This herb can be maintained year-round as a houseplant. Bees do not like feverfew, so do not plant it next to anything that requires bee pollination.

Sun and soil

This herb prefers a rich, well-drained soil, but will adapt to most soils. Water moderately.

When to harvest

Pick or cut leaves before blooming, or cut stems and hang upside down to dry and then remove leaves. Flowers may also be dried for decoration, but most herbalists only use the leaves.

Parts used

The leaves are the only part of the herb used for medicinal purposes.

Medicinal benefits

Feverfew is well-known as a migraine headache remedy, especially in Europe. This herb can also be used as an infusion or tincture.

Flax

Linum usitatissimum

Description

Flax is characterized by a multitude of slender flexible stems with small narrow leaves and small blue flowers. Plants reach a height just shy of 3 feet. Flax is an annual plant native to the region between India and the Mediterranean. Historically, flax in this country was used to make linseed oil and as a fiber to make linen. Flax fibers are among the oldest fiber crop in the world, dating back to the ancient Egyptians.

When to plant

Plant flax seeds in spring after all danger of frost passes. Space flax plants 10 to 12 inches apart.

Sun and soil

Plant flax in full sun. Flax prefers a moist, rich soil. Ideally, compost should be worked into about the top 4 inches prior to planting.

When to harvest

Harvest when 90 percent of the seeds turn brown.

Parts used

Seeds are the only parts of this plant used.

Medicinal benefits

Flax seeds are a great source of healthy omega-3 fatty acids. In addition, they can soothe ear pain, headaches, coughing, joint pain and insomnia.

Garlic

Allium sativum

Description

Originally from central Asia, garlic is grown by dividing its bulb. Garlic is a beneficial herb that offers vitamins A, B, C and E.

When to plant

Garlic can be grown from seeds or cloves, but it is easiest to grow from cloves. Separate the cloves from the bulb, and plant 2 inches deep and 6 inches apart in early spring for fall gathering, or plant in fall for early spring gathering. If planted in the fall, add 3 or 4 inches of mulch. Garlic can be planted about six weeks before the last frost. This plant is easy to grow and is a natural insect repellent.

Sun and soil

This herb prefers a sunny location and moderate watering. Soil should be slightly rich and well composted.

When to harvest

Dig garlic out of the ground when the lower leaves begin to turn brown. After you harvest garlic, save some of the cloves at room temperature in a dark place for the next planting.

Parts used

You can use the cloves, either fresh or dried. When storing fresh garlic, store in a cool, dark place.

Medicinal benefits

Garlic is a powerful infection fighter. Because of its antibacterial properties, it was used during World War I for infected wounds and dysentery. Garlic is also good for the heart, and it lowers blood sugar. Researchers discovered that one garlic clove contains antibacterial properties equal to about 100,000 units of penicillin. The normal dose range for penicillin starts at about 600,000 units, which would be about six cloves of garlic. You can just chew the garlic, or take it in an infusion or tincture. Because of the smell associated with eating garlic, garlic capsules that you can purchase at a natural food store are a popular alternative.

Ginger

Zingiber officinale

Description

Ginger is a perennial, hardy in zones 9 through 11, with spikes of waxy, yellowish flowers. It is characterized as a thick, knotted, light tan underground root. Ginger has been used as a medicinal herb in a variety of cultures around the world, including Arabic, Asian and Indian. It has also been used in China for the last 2,000 years to cure stomach afflictions.

When to plant

Ginger will only grow in tropical regions of the world. Ginger can be planted at anytime in zones 9 through 11. Planting sections of its roots propagates the plant.

Sun and soil

Ginger needs to be planted in a rich, well-worked and evenly moist soil. The plant prefers to grow in either shade or partial shade.

When to harvest

Ideally, ginger should be harvested somewhere between four and nine months after being planted. Once the leaves have died on the ginger plant, the root is ready to be harvested.

Parts used

Roots are the part of this plant used for medicinal purposes.

Medicinal benefits

Ginger can aid in a variety of circulatory and digestive problems. An antioxidant with anti-inflammatory properties, it has been used for fevers, car sickness, dizziness, headaches, nausea and reproductive health. It can be used as a tincture, infusion, compress, medicinal food, ointment, salve and oil, to name a few.

Goldenseal

Hydrastis canadensis

Description

Goldenseal is an endangered plant in the United States because of excessive wild harvesting. It is a popular herb due to its wonderful properties, which contributed to its threatened extinction. Goldenseal has greenish-white flowers that bloom in the spring; bright red berries form from the flower in the summer. It is hardy in zones 5 through 8.

When to plant

Goldenseal is propagated by root divisions in the fall. It is difficult to grow from seeds, but you can buy seeds. They should be stratified in the refrigerator. Sow the seeds in late fall or early spring. The beds should be well shaded to become their permanent home. Goldenseal grows in clumps, so the plants should be spaced about 10 inches apart.

Sun and soil

Goldenseal likes shade and partial shade. It is adaptable to different soils and requires moderate watering.

When to harvest

The underground roots are harvested between 4 and 6 years of age. Dig them out in the fall. Sometimes, the rhizomes show on the surface of the ground. Plants that have rhizomes, such as ivy, usually spread very quickly.

Parts used

The rhizomes, either fresh or dried, of the goldenseal plant are used for healing purposes.

Medicinal benefits

Goldenseal has antibiotic properties and is used for winter illnesses and respiratory complaints. It is also an immune system stimulant. It can be taken as an infusion, tincture, decoction, in capsules, as a suppository, or in a syrup.

Gotu Kola

Centella asiatica

Description

Gotu kola is an annual in North America, but a perennial in tropical climates (zones 8 through 11). It grows 6 to 8 inches high with greenish flowers that sit under the leaves.

When to plant

Gotu kola should be planted once all danger of frost is past. This herb is very difficult to grow from seeds. You can obtain plants from a nursery or order them online. Cuttings need to be kept moist but not too wet. Root divisions are the easiest way to start gotu kola. Separate the parent plant into several divisions and plant. This herb spreads, so leave plenty of room between plants, about 12 to 14 inches. Gotu kola also grows well as a hanging houseplant.

Sun and soil

Gotu kola prefers partial shade to full sun and needs rich, loamy soil. Water moderately.

When to harvest

If grown as a houseplant, you can harvest anytime. Outdoors, it should be harvested during the hot part of the growing season.

Parts used

The parts that grow above the ground can be used.

Medicinal benefits

Gotu kola is good for memory and concentration. Use in an infusion, tincture, or capsule.

Hibiscus

Hibiscus sabdariffa

Description

Native to Asia and the Pacific Islands, hibiscus grows in a variety of regions around the world. If you live in zones 9 or 10, you will be able to grow hibiscus outdoors. If you are in zones 1 through 8, however, you will need to bring the plant indoors to a sunny, warm room during the winter season.

When to plant

Ideally, the hibiscus plant should be planted outdoors 3 to 6 feet apart in late spring in zones 1 through 8. If the hibiscus is being planted in one of these zones, it will need to be moved indoors for winter, as it will not survive the cold temperatures. This can be done by digging it up and replanting it in a pot. An easier way to move the plant around in different seasons would be to keep it planted in a pot and simply move the pot indoors during the colder seasons.

Sun and soil

Hibiscus needs a well-drained soil with a combination of topsoil, sand and peat moss. Place newer plants in partial shade until they are well established. After they are well established, you can move them to a full-sun location.

When to harvest

The flowers of the hibiscus plant should be harvested for use when they are in full bloom by cutting them off the stem with a good pair of gardening shears.

Parts used

The flowers of the hibiscus plant can be used to make a tea.

Medicinal benefits

Hibiscus is high in bioflavonoids and rich in vitamin C. Bioflavonoids are not produced naturally in the human body and instead are absorbed by consuming plants that contain the beneficial water-soluble compound. The bioflavonoids in hibiscus can be useful for treating bruises and swelling, colds, and the flu.

Hops

Humulus lupulus

Description

A perennial plant, hops grow well in zones 4 through 8. Hop vines can grow to 8 feet tall and are characterized by light green **strobiles**, or flower clusters, in late summer. They have been cultivated since about the 8th century A.D. in Bavaria and other parts of Europe. Hops are used primarily as a flavoring and stability agent in beer.

When to plant

Hops are not germinated easily by seed and should, instead, be grown by root divisions or cuttings in the spring or fall. Hops should be planted 3 feet apart.

Sun and soil

Hops will grow in normal to poor soil conditions and prefer partial shade to sun.

When to harvest

The strobiles should be harvested by hand when they are fully developed, usually in late summer to early fall.

Parts used

The strobiles can be used as an infusion, foot or bath soak, tincture, or as a sedative when added to beer.

Medicinal benefits

A hop is a potent medicinal herb that aids in insomnia, hypertension, anxiety and indigestion. It can, however, also temporarily decrease sexual drive in men. As it is a very strong herb, you should use caution. Hops are not recommended for use if you are depressed.

Horseradish

Armoracia rusticana

Description

Horseradish is the thick root of a perennial plant that grows up to 5 feet tall. It has been used for thousands of years and dates back to the ancient

Egyptians, Romans and Greeks. It was commonly used in the Middle Ages for its culinary and medicinal purposes, and it has been cultivated in the United States since the 1800s.

When to plant

Hardy in zones 4 through 9, plant horseradish roots 2 feet apart in early spring.

Sun and soil

Plant horseradish in full sun to promote growth. Horseradish tolerates partial shade, but will not grow as well. It prefers a well-drained, moderately fertile soil.

When to harvest

The root of the horseradish plant will be at its peak flavor one year after planting so try to harvest it the following spring. Unused parts of the root may be replanted to start the process again.

Parts used

The root of this plant is used for medicinal purposes.

Medicinal benefits

Horseradish can be used to treat wounds, skin afflictions and acne. It can be used to relieve headaches and coughs, aid digestion, reduce sweating, increase blood flow, clear congested sinuses and as an antiseptic.

Hyssop

Hyssopus officinalis

Description

Hyssop is a perennial that grows up to 3 feet tall. It grows best in zones 4 to 9. Very small purple or blue tubular flowers form on the tall spikes from midsummer to fall. The leaves are small and lance-shaped.

When to plant

Seeds can be planted about ¼ inch deep a week or two before the last frost. Cuttings for propagation can be taken in late spring or early fall. Plant hyssop 6 to 12 inches apart.

Sun and soil

Hyssop likes well-drained, sandy soils. The top inch of soil should dry between watering, as this plant is susceptible to root rot.

When to harvest

Harvest before the plant blooms in the morning when the dew dries throughout the growing season. You can cut back the entire plant to about 4 inches above the ground and hang upside down to dry, or just pick leaves anytime. Pick the flowers when the blooms are not quite fully open.

Parts used

The leaves are the only part used.

Medicinal benefits

Hyssop was used for cleaning purposes during biblical times because of its antiseptic properties. It can inhibit the growth of the sores caused by the herpes simplex virus. Try the infusion in a compress and place on herpes sores and cold sores. It is also sometimes used to treat coughs and respiratory conditions. Use in a tincture, infusion, decoction, or compress.

Hyssop: One of the Biblical Plants

One of the most well-known plants of the Bible, hyssop is mentioned in both the New and Old testaments. The hyssop plant was used to brush the blood of the sacrificed Passover lamb on the Israelite door frames:

"Then Moses called for all the elders of Israel, and said unto them, Draw out and take you a lamb according to your families, and kill the Passover. And ye shall take a bunch of hyssop, and dip it in the blood that is in the basin, and strike the lintel and the two side posts with the blood that is in the basin; and none of you shall go out at the door of his house until the morning." (Exodus 12:21-22, King James Version)

Hyssop is also mentioned throughout the Bible in a variety of cleansing and purification rituals for lepers, the dead and clearing mold.

Lavender, English

Lavandula angustifolia

Description

Lavender is a perennial that grows up to 3 feet tall. Lavender has very fragrant, slender spikes of blue-purple flowers in midsummer. The leaves are narrow, gray-green or silvery green, and a little hairy. This herb grows best in zones 5 through 8.

When to plant

Start seeds indoors eight weeks before the last frost, and transplant outside after the last frost. They require light for germination. You can also purchase small plants at a nursery.

Sun and soil

Lavender likes full sun, but tolerates partial shade. Soil should be well drained and a bit alkaline. Allow the top inch of soil to dry between watering.

When to harvest

Harvest flower spikes and stems when the flowers are almost completely open. Cut stems several inches below the flower spikes and hang upside down to dry.

Parts used

Aerial parts, either fresh or dried, are the parts of this plant that are used.

Medicinal benefits

The wonderful fragrance of lavender is calming, and sleep pillows can be made from lavender. It is very calming for the nervous system. Use this herb in an infusion, tincture, compress, or cream.

CASE STUDY

David Catherman
Sleepy Bee Lavender
424 Matson Hill Road
South Glastonbury, CT 06073
860-978-5032
www.sleepybeelavender.com
Drcath@tiac.net

David Catherman set out to develop a rural residential lavender farm. He has been perfecting his "lifestyle hobby" since 2003. Catherman enjoys growing lavender for the "personal satisfaction in creating a beautiful landscape, gaining knowledge about the cultivation and processing of a natural product, and replicating the agricultural lifestyle and business model of running a lavender farm." In addition, Catherman sells dried lavender craft items like sachets, pin cushions, eye pillows and essential oils via his website and at local farmers markets.

Catherman grows the lavender on his farm in parallel rows of raised beds. To successfully grow lavender, he ensures that his soil pH is between 6 and 8. If your soil is too acidic, he suggests that you add lime to raise the pH. For proper drainage, Catherman recommends adding sand and gravel. He warns that lavender does not respond well to nitrogen-based fertilizers. Instead, he suggests using a small amount of aged manure compost mixed in with the native soil prior to planting. When it comes time to harvest lavender, small plots can easily be cut by hand using a sickle — a tool with a short handle and semi circular blade — and special mechanical harvesters can successfully cut larger plots for harvest.

Here is advice Catherman offers to anyone looking to start growing, harvesting and using healing herbs:

• Decide what you want to do. Don't overextend yourself or underestimate the time commitment required.

- Have your soil tested and evaluate the results against the cultivation requirements of the plants you want to grow.

- Research all that you can about the requirements of each herb from multiple sources, and amend your soil accordingly.

- Decide if the time, physical effort, and costs required make the venture worth pursuing.

Proceed with caution, as some people can have allergic or adverse reactions to certain herbs, especially in concentrated forms such as pure, undiluted essential oils.

Lemon Balm

Melissa officinalis

Description

Lemon balm is a perennial that grows best in zones 4 through 9, reaching a height of 1 to 2 feet tall. It has clusters of white, tubular flowers that bloom in summer. The leaves are a bright green and have toothed edges. It dies back during winter months.

When to plant

Start seeds indoors eight weeks before the last frost and transplant outdoors about a week before the last frost. They can also be sown directly in the garden two weeks before the last frost. Divide the plants in the spring and replant. Space lemon balm plants 12 to 15 inches apart.

Sun and soil

This herb prefers full sun in the northern regions of the United States and partial or filtered shade in the southern regions. Lemon balm likes well-drained, moderately fertile soil.

When to harvest

Leaves may be harvested any time in the morning after the dew dries for immediate use, or you can harvest the upper half of the plant and hang upside down to dry. The plant can be harvested at any time throughout the growing season; it will regenerate and give you many cuttings during the season.

Parts used

The parts that grow above ground, either fresh or dried, can be used in any number of medicinal remedies.

Medicinal benefits

Lemon balm is good for the digestive tract, winter illnesses like colds and the flu, and strengthening the immune system. This is an herb children can take for winter illnesses too. It is a very good stress reliever. Use as a tea, infusion, decoction, or tincture. It can also be used as food in salads, stuffing, and over fish and chicken.

Lemon Verbena

Aloysia triphylla

Description

Lemon verbena is a perennial that grows up to 2 feet tall. It grows best in zones 9 and 10, but can be grown indoors in containers in colder climates. It has spikes of tiny lavender flowers where the leaves join the stems. The leaves are narrow and pointed.

When to plant

If you can find the seeds, they are very difficult to grow. It is best to purchase a plant, and you should be able to find one without difficulty at your garden center. You can then take cuttings in late spring or early summer. Cuttings are also a bit difficult and you will need to use a rooting hormone. A **rooting hormone** will stimulate the roots to grow, and it can be purchased at any store that has garden supplies. The cuttings require temperatures of 65 to 70 degrees at night and 80 to 90 degrees in the daytime. They need good air circulation and consistent moisture. Transplant outdoors when the weather remains warm and bring the plants indoors before frost.

Sun and soil

This herb prefers rich soil, but is adaptable if given enough water. It likes sun or partial shade and should be fed fish emulsion and liquid seaweed fertilizers because this will immediately give needed nutrients to the plant. Both types of fertilizers are readily available at your local garden center or home improvement store. They are also available online.

When to harvest

Leaves and stems may be harvested anytime after the plant reaches 8 inches tall. Cut the aerial parts in the summer. Hang upside down to dry, and then strip leaves from the stems and discard the stems.

Parts used

You can use the leaves and flowers, either fresh or dried.

Medicinal benefits

Lemon verbena is used as a calming tea and a sleep herb. You can also add leaves to salad dressings and beverages.

Lemongrass

Cymbopogon citratus

Description

Lemongrass is a tender perennial best grown in zones 8 through 11. Native to Sri Lanka and Seychelles, lemongrass is characterized by strong, green shoots.

When to plant

Lemongrass can be grown from seed in late spring after all danger of frost passes. Lemongrass is a perennial if grown in tropical climates. If you are attempting to grow lemongrass in cooler regions, you will want to treat it like an annual or move it to a warm, sunny indoor location during the winter as it will not survive outdoors. Plants need to be spaced 36 to 40 inches apart.

Sun and soil

Lemongrass likes to be planted in a moist or sandy soil. It prefers full sun, but can also survive in partial shade to full shade.

When to harvest

Lemongrass is ideally harvested in mid to late summer by cutting of its branches and shoots.

Parts used

The green shoots of this plant are used for medicinal purposes.

Medicinal benefits

Lemongrass is an anti-inflammatory herb that supports a healthy digestive tract and can be used in a tincture, herbal honey, or infusion.

Licorice

Glycyrrhiza glabra

Description

Native to southern Europe and parts of Asia, licorice is a tender perennial that grows best in zones 9 through 11. It can grow to a height of 4 to 5 feet and puts forth lavender and white flowers.

When to plant

Before planting in late spring, licorice seeds need to be stratified for several weeks. Prior to planting the seeds, they need to be scarified and soaked in warm water for two hours. Licorice dies back each winter and returns late spring. Ideally, you want to space licorice plants 2 feet apart.

Sun and soil

Licorice should be grown in well-drained soil in full sun to partial shade.

When to harvest

Licorice should be harvested in either the spring or fall, but not until its third year of growth.

Parts used

Rhizomes are used for medicinal purposes.

Medicinal benefits

Licorice can be used as a tincture, syrup, lozenge, powder, or food to assist in winter illnesses, boost immunity, provide adrenal gland support, and improve respiratory and digestive tract health.

Lovage

Levisticum officinale

Description

Lovage is a perennial that grows best in zones 5 to 8. It can reach a height of 3 feet and has umbels of tiny white flowers in summer. The leaves resemble celery leaves in taste and appearance. The plant dies back in the winter.

When to plant

Seeds must be stratified for one to two weeks before sowing indoors, and germination takes about two weeks. This plant clumps, so transplant it outdoors, spaced about 24 inches apart. Seeds can be sown directly outdoors just before the last spring frost. You can buy plants at the nursery and plant outdoors just before the last frost.

Sun and soil

This herb must have well-drained, moist soil and needs mulch in the spring. Lovage prefers partial shade.

When to harvest

Leaves can be harvested anytime during the growing season before the plant flowers. Harvest entire ripe seed heads in the late summer. The roots should be harvested in the spring or fall.

Parts used

Roots, leaves, stems and seeds can be used, either fresh or dried.

Medicinal benefits

Lovage is an antiseptic and can be applied to wounds using a strong infusion. Lovage tea stimulates digestion. It is very good for winter illnesses like a cold and the flu, and for respiratory tract issues. Use as an infusion, decoction, tincture, or medicinal food. Lovage tastes like celery and can be used in recipes calling for celery. The fresh leaves can be used in salads.

Marshmallow

Althaea officinalis

Description

This perennial grows best in zones 5 through 8. In summer, it grows to a height of 3 to 4 feet with pale pink flowers all the way up the stalk. It has gray-green leaves that are toothed and hairy. The stem is also hairy.

When to plant

Seeds can be planted outside in early spring depending on your location, or they can be started indoors and planted outside in mid- to late spring. It grows in clumps and should be spaced 12 inches apart.

Sun and soil

Marshmallow likes sun or partial shade and moderate watering. It prefers loamy soil.

When to harvest

The roots of marshmallow are harvested in either the spring or fall. The leaves and flowers can be handpicked any time.

Parts used

The roots, leaves and flowers of this herb can all be used, either fresh or dried.

Medicinal benefits

A confection called marshmallow was made from the roots of this herb in the 1800s. The roots were cooked with sugar and whipped. Although the modern version of the marshmallow contains none of this plant, this is where it originated. Marshmallow is very soothing to the gastrointestinal tract and throat. Some herbalists rely on it for the urinary tract also. It can be used as an infusion, tincture, syrup, lozenge, or as medicinal food.

Milk Thistle

Silybum marianum

Description

Milk thistle has very pretty, spiny purple flowers in the late summer. This plant is very prickly and grows 2 to 3 feet tall, mainly in zones 6 through 9.

When to plant

Milk thistle seeds are best sown directly outdoors when the weather is settled, meaning you are sure spring has finally arrived. It grows in clumps, so space the plant 12 to 15 inches apart.

Sun and soil

This was originally a Mediterranean plant, so it loves full sun and light watering. There are no special soil requirements for this milk thistle.

When to harvest

Harvest the seeds when they turn brown. Gloves are required when harvesting to protect your hands because of this plant's prickly nature. Snip off seed heads and place in a shallow box. With gloves on, dislodge the seeds from the pods and then separate the seeds. Discard everything else.

Parts used

You can use the seeds, either fresh or dried.

Medicinal benefits

Milk thistle is a well-known liver tonic; it protects the liver and renews liver cells. It is used in the treatment of hepatitis and jaundice and to treat the side effects of chemotherapy. It is also used to for those afflicted with Crohn's disease, irritable bowel syndrome, and gallstones, and is believed to slow the progress of Parkinson's disease. Use the seeds in teas, tinctures, and capsules.

Mint

Peppermint: *Mentha piperita*
Spearmint: *Mentha spicata*
Apple mint: *Mentha suaveolens*
Pennyroyal*: *Mentha pulegium*

Description

Mints are perennial herbs that can grow up to 2 feet tall, depending on the species, and they grow best in zones 5 through 9. Mints can also be grown indoors on a windowsill. They have spikes of tiny purple, white, or pink flowers, and the leaves are many shades of green, most with toothed edges. The plants die back over the winter. There are many different varieties of mints.

When to plant

It is best to buy small plants from a nursery and plant outdoors from early spring through summer. You can also keep mints indoors for handy use in cooking or beverages. Mints do spread quickly, so you might want to plant in containers and bury the container, or grow mints on your patio in large pots.

Sun and soil

Mints like moist soils and partial or filtered shade.

When to harvest

Gather leaves any time after the plants reach 6 to 8 inches. For drying, cut stems 4 inches above the soil surface and hang upside down to dry.

Parts used

The leaves are the only part used.

Medicinal benefits

Mints are good for an upset stomach and they can help relieve gas. Peppermint and spearmint promote sleep. Mint is often used in an infusion and is also used to make delicious teas.

*Pennyroyal is primarily sold as an ornamental herb due to its high level of toxicity. It is recommended that only experts use and grow this dangerous herb.

Motherwort

Leonurus cardiaca

Description

Motherwort is a perennial that grows best in zones 4 through 8. It grows 2 to 4 feet tall with small lavender flowers.

When to plant

Seeds need to be stratified for several weeks and then sown directly outdoors in mid-spring. Seeds germinate in about two weeks. This herb grows in clumps and should be spaced 15 to 20 inches apart.

Sun and soil

This plant can be grown in full sun or partial shade. There are no special soil needs, and it should be watered moderately.

When to harvest

The aerial parts can be harvested anytime.

Parts used

The only parts of the motherwort plant that are used are the parts that grow above ground, either fresh or dried.

Medicinal benefits

Motherwort is often given after childbirth to help recovery. It is also used to encourage normal menstrual cycles. Motherwort is a good heart tonic and is also used for some nervous conditions. Use as an infusion, tincture, or in capsules.

Mullein

Verbascum thapsus

Description

Mullein is a biennial that will grow to 5 or 6 feet tall. A stalk of individual yellow flowers will emerge in the second year, and the leaves are large, hairy, and tongue-shaped. It grows best in zones 3 through 9.

When to plant

Mullein is easily grown from seeds in light sandy soil. To plant outside, sow after all danger of frost passes. It grows in clumps and reseeds itself. Plants should be spaced about 15 inches apart.

Sun and soil

Mullein likes full sun and light to moderate watering.

When to harvest

Harvest roots in the fall of the first year, or in the spring of the second. Leaves can be handpicked any time after the dew dries, and flowers can be handpicked during blooming. Harvest flowers by snipping off the upper 3 to 6 inches of the stalk when it is full of buds and just about ready to bloom. Weevils inhabit the plant so it is a good idea to lay the plant material in the shade for several hours to allow the weevils to exit.

Parts used

The roots, leaves and flowers, either fresh or dried, can be used from this plant for medicinal purposes.

Medicinal benefits

The roots are used for the urinary tract, and the leaves and flowers are used for the respiratory tract. Mullein is good for coughs and sore throats. For hemorrhoids, apply a strong cold compress. This herb can be used as a tea, infusion, or tincture.

Nasturtium

Tropaeolum majus

Description

Nasturtium is an annual that grows to 1 foot tall and then produces a vine up to 6 feet long. Various colored, funnel-shaped flowers bloom from summer through fall. The flowers have five petals and are about 2 inches across. The leaves are round with wavy margins.

When to plant

Nasturtiums are easy to grow. Sow seeds in the garden around the time of the last frost. They can be started indoors in newspaper or peat pots and transplanted after all chance of frost passes. Space plants 12 inches apart.

Sun and soil

Full sun will make the nasturtiums produce more flowers. They like well-drained, moderately fertile soil.

When to harvest

Pick individual leaves when the plants are 6 inches tall. Flowers should be picked as they open. You can collect the seedpods when they are a little more than ¼ inch in diameter. Cut entire stems of leaves and flowers.

Parts used

Fresh leaves and flowers from this plant are used as a medicinal food.

Medicinal benefits

Nasturtiums are loaded with vitamins and have antiseptic properties. When eaten raw, they help fight fungal and bacterial infections. Use the leaves and flowers in salads as a medicinal food.

Nettle

Urtica dioica

Description

This plant is a perennial, grown in zones 5 through 9, that grows to 2 to 4 feet. It has tiny cream-colored flowers in the summer and has heart-shaped leaves with hairs that are actually hollow needles. It is sometimes called "stinging nettle" — and for good reason. Gloves and protective clothing should always be worn around this herb.

When to plant

Nettle grows easily from seed in almost any soil. Sow directly in the garden in early spring. Remember to wear gloves when working with seedlings. Nettle spreads, so plants should be spaced about 12 inches apart.

Sun and soil

Nettle will grow in full sun, partial shade, or full shade. It prefers a soil that is high in organic matter, and it requires moderate to heavy watering.

When to harvest

Harvest nettle any time before flowering. Be sure to wear heavy gloves and use scissors or snips. Dried nettles do not sting.

Parts used

Use the aerial parts of this plant, fresh or dried, for their medicinal assistance.

Medicinal benefits

Nettles are rich in vitamins and minerals and helpful to the whole body. They aid male and female reproductive health, can help with urinary tract problems and respiratory complaints, and can also be used to help allergy symptoms. They are used in an infusion, tincture, cream and as a medicinal food. Nettle is recommended as a tonic to strengthen the entire body.

Oat

Avena Sativa

Description

Oat is a grain that is primarily grown as a food for human and animal consumption. Originating in the Mediterranean and in China, oat is grown today in the United States, Russia, Canada, Turkey, Spain, the United Kingdom, Germany and Iraq. Oat looks like long stalks of grass with seedpods that form near the top. It is a self-seeding annual and may return the following season.

When to plant

Sow seeds directly outdoors in early to late spring.

Sun and soil

Oat thrives in full sun, preferring a dry soil, and will not need to be watered very often.

When to harvest

The seeds and stalks should be harvested when the plant is still green to ensure maximum benefits of the plant.

Parts used

The seeds and grassy stalks of the oat can be used for medicinal purposes.

Medicinal benefits

In addition to the heart health benefits of consuming oats as a food, oats are high in protein and decrease LDL, or bad, cholesterol. Oat straw can also be used to assist in combating fatigue that comes with diseases like multiple sclerosis and chronic neurological pain. It is also used in a variety of skin care products due to its calming nature.

Onion

Allium cepa

Description

Onions are edible bulbs that are part of the allium family of plants. Chives, leeks, garlic and shallots are all members of this family. Onion bulbs are round, sometimes oblong, and can be either slightly bitter tasting or sweet. Onions grow below the ground and sprout tubular green stalks.

When to plant

Onions can be planted in early spring as soon as the soil can easily be worked.

Sun and soil

Plant onions in full sun to maximize their growing potential. Place onion bulbs 3 to 6 inches apart. Onions prefer a moist, loamy soil, but will thrive in a variety of conditions.

When to harvest

Onion bulbs are ready to harvest when about half of the green stalks have tipped over. Gently push the remaining tops over and allow them to dry out for a few days before harvesting the onion. Rather than pulling the bulbs out of the ground, dig them out with a small shovel. The tops can be braided together to hang the onions for drying.

Parts used

The bulb portion of the onion is used for food and medicinal purposes.

Medicinal benefits

Onions have been found to inhibit the growth of cancer cells, combat heart disease, lower blood pressure and stimulate the immune system. Onions can be used medicinally as a food ingredient or as an essential oil.

Oregano

Origanum vulgare

Description

Oregano is a perennial that grows best in zones 5 through 9. It grows to 2 feet tall with tiny lavender flowers during the summer and can have leaves that are either toothed or smooth on the edges.

When to plant

Oregano is very aromatic. If you buy the plants at the nursery, you can be confident you will get the flavor you want. You can start from seed by putting three to five seeds in a small starter pot about eight weeks before the last frost. The seedlings can be planted in the garden a week before the date of the estimated last frost. Space plants 12 inches apart.

Sun and soil

Oregano likes full sun and well-drained soil. The top inch of the soil should dry out between watering.

When to harvest

Oregano can be harvested anytime during the growing season. Cut from the stem and hang upside down to dry, or cut small sprigs for immediate use.

Parts used

Use the aerial parts, either fresh or dry.

Medicinal benefits

Oregano tea, made by boiling the leaves in water, can help clear nasal passages and ease sore throats. It is good for winter illnesses and has been traditionally used to support a healthy digestive system. Oregano is also a strong antiseptic for minor skin injuries.

Parsley

Petroselinum crispum

Description

Parsley is a biennial herb that can grow up to 1 foot tall. Parsley has a bright green stem, ruffled leaves and can produce small white flowers. Native to Europe and the eastern Mediterranean, parsley is a popular salad and food garnish.

When to plant

Seeds can be started indoors ten to 12 weeks prior to the last frost. Or, start outdoors three to four weeks prior to the last frost. Plant the seeds 6 to 8 inches apart. Seeds can take up to three weeks to germinate.

Sun and soil

Parsley prefers a rich, moist soil and direct sunlight.

When to harvest

Leaves can be cut from the outer stalks of the plant at any time during the growing season. The seeds should be harvested just before they start to fall to the ground naturally.

Parts used

The leaves of the parsley plant are primarily used in cooking. Both the root and seeds of the parsley plant can also be used.

Medicinal benefits

The seeds of the parsley plant have a diuretic property and can be used in the treatment of gout, arthritis and rheumatism. Parsley root can be used to treat flatulence.

Caution

Parsley is a safe herb at normal consumption levels, but excessive amounts of the seeds can become toxic. Avoid parsley seed if you have kidney disease or are pregnant.

Passionflower

Passiflora incarnata

Description

Passionflower is a perennial that can grow 8 feet tall or higher and is native to the southeastern United States. Passionflower is hardy in zones 5 through 9. It has dull green leaves and very exotic white and lavender flowers that bloom in late spring through summer. The flowers produce a yellow or orange edible fruit that is about the size of an egg. Passionflower has climbing tendrils that need a trellis.

When to plant

This plant grows fairly easily from seeds, cuttings, or root divisions. When starting from seed, plant after all danger of frost passes. If starting from cuttings, use a rooting hormone to stimulate root growth, and keep the cuttings warm and moist until rooting. Once rooted, plant directly in the garden after all danger of frost has passed. Rooting hormones can be found at your local garden or home improvement center. Space plants 18 inches apart.

Sun and soil

Plant passionflower in an area of shade or partial shade because it cannot tolerate full sun. Passionflower likes slightly acidic soil that is rich and loamy, and this plant requires heavy watering.

When to harvest

All aerial parts may be harvested, including the fruit, anytime during the growing season.

Parts used

Aerial parts, either fresh or dried, are used.

Medicinal benefits

Passionflower is known as a strong sedative and nerve tonic. Make a tea of the dried leaves to help you relax or fall asleep. It is used as an infusion or tincture.

Plantain

Plantago major, P. lanceolata, P. media

Description

Plantain is a perennial that ranges in height from 8 to 20 inches tall. It has tiny white flowers on a stalk.

When to plant

It is very easy to grow plantain from seed, and plants will usually sprout in one to two weeks. Start indoors in early spring and transplant outdoors in late spring. If starting outdoors, plant in early to mid-spring. Plantain grows in clumps, so space plants about 12 inches apart.

Sun and soil

Plantain likes full sun or partial shade, and it likes moderate water. It has no special soil requirements.

When to harvest

The whole plant is harvested from spring to fall. Dig this plant up from the roots. Some people like the roots because they feel all the medicinal qualities are in the roots. However, there are many who use the entire plant. Seeds can be harvested when they are ready.

Parts used

The whole plant can be used including roots, leaves, and seeds, either fresh or dried.

Medicinal benefits

Placing a plantain leaf directly on a foot blister and taping it to the body will soothe the irritation and promote healing. It is also good for stopping minor bleeding and relieving insect bites and stings. Use as a salve, infusion, or tincture.

Pumpkin

Cucurbita pepo

Description

Pumpkin is an annual plant with twisting stems, yellow flowers and large orange-colored fruit. Pumpkin can be found worldwide and has been used medicinally throughout a variety of cultures.

When to plant

To promote seed germination, soak pumpkin seeds in warm water for 24 hours prior to planting. Seeds can either be sown directly in the ground outside or started indoors. When planting directly outdoors, plant seeds once danger of frost has passed 1 to 1½ inches deep in small hills spaced 6 to 8 inches apart. Pumpkins will need plenty of room to spread out as their vines can grow up to 30 feet long.

Sun and soil

Plant pumpkins where they will receive at least six hours of sunlight a day in average soil. Keep pumpkin plants relatively moist.

When to harvest

Pumpkins are ready to be harvested in the fall when the stems and leaves begin to dry out and brown.

Parts used

The pulp and seeds of the pumpkin fruit are used for medicinal purposes, food consumption and decoration.

Medicinal benefits

Pumpkin can be used as a de-worming agent. The seeds are a diuretic and are also valuable in the early treatment of prostate enlargement. The fruit pulp can be used as a decoction to relieve intestinal inflammation. The pulp can also be used to soothe burns.

Red Clover

Trifolium pratense

Description

Red clover is a perennial that grows up to 15 inches and is hardy in zones 5 through 9. It has large, pink blossoms in the summer.

When to plant

Sow seeds directly outdoors in early spring and they will germinate in about ten days. Red clover grows in clumps, so space the plants about 12 inches apart.

Sun and soil

No special soil is needed, and this plant loves full sun or partial shade. Water red clover moderately.

When to harvest

The flower blossoms are the only part of red clover that is harvested. To dry this herb, it must be picked when the dew is still on the blossoms. Lay the flowers on a screen to dry; when they are fully dried, they will have a deep purple-red color.

Parts used

The blossoms are the only part of this herb that is used.

Medicinal benefits

Red clover supports the immune system. It is also often used for women's health and children's health concerns. Use as a tea, infusion, or tincture; it can also be made into a salve.

Red Raspberry

Rubus idaeus

Description

The red raspberry is a woody shrub perennial that can grow to 6 feet. The stems, or canes, of the plant are woody with prickers, which are sharp protrusions growing from the stem. The raspberry bush has pale green leaves, white flowers, and red berries. The raspberry is native to Europe and Asia, but is now grown worldwide.

When to plant

Raspberries can be planted in either spring or fall. Plant new canes 3 feet apart in rows, and water until well established. Raspberries will need to be pruned on a yearly basis to keep the plants from growing wild and becoming unruly.

Sun and soil

Raspberries prefer full sun, but will also tolerate partly shady, woodland areas. They prefer a rich, moist and well-drained soil.

When to harvest

The fruits can be harvested when they are plump and red. Harvest the leaves throughout the season as they are needed.

Parts used

Both the leaves and the fruit of the raspberry plant are used for food consumption and for medicinal purposes.

Medicinal benefits

The leaves of the raspberry plant can be used during labor as a tea to quicken the childbirth process. Raspberry leaves can also be used as a decoction to help relieve diarrhea. The leaves can also be used as an astringent mouthwash to alleviate mouth sores. The fruit of the raspberry plant is nutritionally beneficial as a source for vitamins A, B and C.

Rosemary

Rosmarinus officinalis

Description

This is a perennial that grows best in zones 8 through 11. It will grow to a height of 3 feet or more. Bluish-purple flowers bloom on rosemary when the nights become cooler. The leaves of the rosemary plant are spiky in nature.

When to plant

It is best to buy small rosemary plants because rosemary seeds grow very slowly. Keep plants indoors until night temperatures are up to 55 degrees. You can take cuttings from plants in late summer.

Sun and soil

Rosemary likes full sun and well-drained soil. It only needs light to moderate watering.

When to harvest

Stems and leaves can be harvested anytime during the growing season.

Parts used

Aerial parts, fresh or dried, are the only parts used.

Medicinal benefits

Rosemary is an excellent source of antioxidants. It is very beneficial for the immune system and is also suggested for the digestive tract. Because it is an aromatic, rosemary tea is good for clearing congestion.

Sage

Salvia officinalis

Description

Native to the Mediterranean, sage is a popular culinary herb that also has a multitude of health benefits. Sage is characterized by green leafy stalks with spikes of purple flowers. Hardy in zones 5 through 9, sage grows up to 2 feet high and 3 feet wide.

When to plant

Sage can be started directly from seed. Sage can grow outdoors in the garden, but will also do well grown in a container indoors. Sage can be planted or sown directly in the outdoor garden one week prior to the last frost date. Plant at least 36 inches apart to allow for full growth.

Sun and soil

Sage prefers a warm, sunny location but does not like extreme heat. It is not picky about soil, but like most herbs, it does require well-draining soil.

When to harvest

Sage should not be harvested until its second year of growth. After the first year, harvest sage as needed throughout the season.

Parts used

The leaves of the sage plant are used fresh and dried for culinary and healing purposes. In addition to being used to flavor meals, sage can also be used as a medicinal tea.

Medicinal benefits

Sage can be used to treat a variety of ailments including depression, anxiety, circulation problems and menopausal concerns. Sage also has an antiseptic property, which is beneficial in treating laryngitis when used as a gargle. Additionally, sage can be used to cleanse the mouth and teeth.

Self-Heal

Prunella vulgaris

Description

Self-heal is a perennial that grows 8 to 10 inches with flowers varying in color from purple to pink to white. It blooms early and the leaves are long and narrow. Native to Europe and Asia, self-heal grows best in zones 4 through 9.

When to plant

Seeds should be stratified for about a month, and then you should sow them indoors. Seeds should germinate after about three weeks. Move this plant outdoors in late spring and space 6 to 9 inches apart.

Sun and soil

Self-heal prefers full sun or partial shade and a humus soil. Water moderately.

When to harvest

Harvest the aerial parts while the plant is in bloom.

Parts used

Aerial parts are used, either fresh or dried.

Medicinal benefits

Self-heal in a weak infusion is used as an eyewash for pinkeye or sties. It is taken internally as a tea for fevers and diarrhea. Research shows it offers antibacterial action against some types of damaging bacteria, which supports its use as an antibiotic and for hard-to-heal wounds and diseases.

Sheep Sorrel

Rumex acetosella

Description

Sheep sorrel is a perennial that grows up to 1 foot tall and is hardy in zones 3 through 9. It has reddish-purple flower stalks that appear in late summer.

When to plant

Sheep sorrel is easy to grow, and you can sow seeds directly outdoors in mid-spring. The seeds will germinate in seven to ten days. It spreads, so space plants about 12 inches apart.

Sun and soil

Sheep sorrel likes full sun and light to moderate watering. There are no special soil requirements.

When to harvest

Aerial parts are harvested in the summer.

Parts used

Aerial parts, fresh or dried, are used.

Medicinal benefits

Sheep sorrel is traditionally used for the immune system and lymphatic system. Use as an infusion, tincture, or capsule.

Shepherd's Purse

Capsella bursa-pastoris

Description

Shepherd's purse is an annual that grows to 2 feet tall and has little white flowers that blossom in late spring to early summer. This plant is a member of the mustard family.

When to plant

This is an early spring herb, so sow seeds outdoors in late fall. This plant grows in clumps and should be spaced 10 inches apart.

Sun and soil

Shepherd's purse likes full sun and well-drained soil. It requires only moderate watering.

When to harvest

Harvest aerial parts when the plant is in full bloom from spring through fall.

Parts used

Flowering aerial parts, fresh or dried, are the parts that are used.

Medicinal benefits

Shepherd's purse contains substances that help blood clot, so traditionally it has been used to treat bleeding. It also has some antiseptic properties. Use in an infusion, tincture, or capsule.

Skullcap

Scutellaria lateriflora

Description

This herb gets its name from its bluish-purple flowers that resemble little skulls wearing hats. It is a perennial that grows to 2 feet tall and is hardy in zones 4 through 8.

When to plant

Sow indoors early. Germination takes about two weeks. You can transplant skullcap outside after all danger of frost passes. This herb grows in clumps, so space plants about 12 inches apart.

Sun and soil

Plant this herb in full sun or partial shade. Skullcap likes well-drained and moist soil.

When to harvest

Harvest aerial parts when skullcap is in full bloom, starting about 3 inches above the ground.

Parts used

Flowering aerial parts, fresh or dry, should be used.

Medicinal benefits

Skullcap is one of the best herbs for calming nervous tension. It is used to relieve stress and anxiety. Use as a tincture or infusion.

St. John's Wort

Hypericum perforatum

Description

A long-time remedy used to treat emotional disorders, St. John's wort got its name because the flowers bloom on the plant around the time of St. John the Baptist's birthday. The word "wort" is an Old English term meaning "plant." The plant has been primarily cultivated for its medicinal uses, but is also an ornamental perennial herb growing to 32 inches in zones 3 through 9, with pretty little yellow flowers on green stems.

When to plant

Ideally, new plants should be started indoors. After the last frost in your zone, start seeds indoors by planting three to four seeds per small pot to ensure proper germination. Place the pots in a dark, warm room and keep moist until they sprout. Once the seedlings have grown two leaves, harden them off by placing them outdoors in a sunny spot for a couple of hours each day to get used to the outdoor temperatures. Return them inside and increase the amount of time spent outdoors by an hour daily until you reach six hours of sun a day. Transplant into an outdoor garden bed when the seedlings have gotten accustomed to six hours of sun and have reached 2 inches tall. Space plants 16 to 18 inches apart. In addition to growing from seed, St. John's wort can be propagated by root division.

Sun and soil

St. John's wort is a relatively simple plant to cultivate and can tolerate a variety of growing conditions ranging from full sun to shade. Though it prefers a light, moist soil, St. John's wort will also grow well in a sandier, heavy soil.

When to harvest

The flowering tops of the herb can be harvested during the summer season when they are in bloom.

Parts used

The flowering tops of St. John's wort are used for medicinal purposes in oils, teas, creams and tinctures.

Medicinal benefits

St. John's wort is a medicinally effective herb that has been used to treat a variety of ailments including depression, anxiety, obsessive compulsive disorder and even ear pain. It has also been used to treat skin conditions like eczema, burns and hemorrhoids. St. John's wort can be used in a variety of forms including tablets, liquid extract, tea, ointments and lotions.

Stevia

Stevia rebaudiana

Description

With delicate white flowers that bloom on and off throughout the season, stevia is an annual that grows 12 to 15 inches tall. In zones 9 through 11, it can be grown as a perennial. It is native to tropical and subtropical regions of North and South America, specifically Paraguay and Brazil. Stevia is well known as a sweetener for foods and medicines.

When to plant

Stevia can be grown from cuttings or seed, but it might be easiest to purchase a seedling as the herb can be difficult to germinate. Stevia can be grown outdoors in tropical regions all year long, but should be considered an annual and planted during hot summer months in other regions. Space stevia plants 18 to 24 inches apart.

Sun and soil

Stevia grows best in a rich, moist, humus soil, which is created by adding compost. Stevia can tolerate full sun as well as shade.

When to harvest

Leaves and flowers can be harvested at any time throughout the growing season.

Parts used

The leaves, stems and flowers of the stevia plant can all be used. They are especially useful frozen in ice cubes for drinks, or as tinctures and powders.

Medicinal benefits

In addition to being a natural sweetener, stevia can also support a healthy digestive tract.

Strawberry, Virginian

Fragaria virginiana

Description

Low-growing green foliage with delicate yellow-centered white flowers and red berries characterize this well-loved summer-bearing perennial plant. Hardy in zones 3 through 8, the strawberry is a nutritionally beneficial plant that also contains a high level of anti-inflammatory characteristics. Strawberry plants are part of the rose family and grow in the wild. They are also easily cultivated. Three varieties of strawberry plants are available: June-bearing, ever-bearing and day-neutral. June-bearing strawberry plants produce large-sized strawberries once in late spring. Ever-bearing plants produce a harvest of medium-sized strawberries in spring and in autumn. Day-neutral plants produce small strawberries throughout the growing season.

When to plant

Strawberry plants can be grown in a variety of ways, including in a bed, in hanging baskets, or in pots. The plants are most easily started by purchasing seedlings from a nursery or garden center. Strawberry can be planted in either spring or fall. Space plants 12 to 18 inches apart in beds.

Sun and soil

The strawberry plant prefers full sun, but is also tolerable of partial shade. Strawberry plants prefer a well-drained, moist and nutrient-rich soil.

When to harvest

The leaves of the plant can be harvested at any time throughout the growing season. The berries of the plant should be harvested when ripe and fully red.

Parts used

The fruits produced by the strawberry plant are used as a nutritious edible food. In addition, the leaves of the strawberry plant can be used to make a tea.

Medicinal benefits

The berries of the strawberry plant contain a high level of nutritional benefits including vitamins B and C, manganese, potassium, folate and dietary fiber. Strawberries can also help whiten teeth. Because of their high level of anti-inflammatory properties, strawberries are helpful for people with osteoarthritis, asthma, rheumatoid arthritis and cancer.

Sunflower

Helianthus annus

Description

Native to North America, Peru and Mexico, the sunflower is an annual plant that grows in varying heights on long green stalks. Ranging in shades from pale yellow to deep red, certain varieties of sunflower can grow to

20 feet tall with blooms over 2 feet wide. The center of the blooms on a sunflower plant have seeds that range in color from solid black to dark brown, or gray with white stripes. Sunflower plants were used by Native Americans to create dyes and medicinally as an ointment, and the seeds were ground to make breads.

When to plant

Ideally, sunflower plants are best started by seed directly in the garden in the springtime. When choosing to start seeds indoors, use individual pots made of peat that can be planted directly in the ground, as sunflower plants do not like to be disturbed once started. Seed spacing will vary depending on sunflower variety. To determine proper spacing, read the back of the seed packet. Once planted, cover with a screen to ensure the birds and squirrels do not eat the seeds.

Sun and soil

Sunflower plants prefer full sun and will turn their blooms to face the direction of the rising sun in the east. Sunflower will grow best in average to rich soils. Avoid planting in sandy soils, as the roots need a sturdy place to grow to support the stem and flower bloom.

When to harvest

Sunflower seeds should be harvested once the flower begins to die back and lose some of its leaves. Cut off the plant's stalk a few inches below the flower bloom and hang upside down to dry in a well-ventilated area. As soon as the flowers have completely dried, the seeds can be extracted by gently pulling them out with your fingers or by rubbing two seed heads together. Harvest roots in the fall when the growing season is over.

Parts used

The seeds and roots of the sunflower plant can all be used for their edible medicinal properties.

Medicinal benefits

Sunflower seeds contain high levels of vitamin E. Vitamin E, due to its anti-inflammatory properties, can reduce the symptoms of asthma and osteoarthritis and decrease the severity of hot flashes. Also a good source of selenium, sunflower seeds can inhibit the production of cancer cells. A tea made from the leaves of the sunflower plant can treat high fevers, assist with lung ailments and stop diarrhea. The root of the sunflower plant can be made into a poultice to treat snake and spider bites.

Tarragon

Artemisia dracunculus

Description

Derived from the French word "estragon," meaning "little dragon," tarragon is a well-known culinary herb that offers several medicinal properties as well. Tarragon is a perennial herb that grows 2 to 3 feet tall and is hardy in zones 4 through 8. Tarragon is a shrub-like plant with slender stalks and yellow flowers. It is native to the Unites States, Asia and Siberia.

When to plant

Tarragon starts best through root propagation. Purchasing a plant already started at your local nursery or garden center is the best way to get started with this plant in your garden. Tarragon can be planted directly in the ground, in a raised bed, or in a container in spring after all danger of frost has passed. Plants should be spaced 18 to 24 inches apart.

Sun and soil

Tarragon prefers full sun to grow well, but will also tolerate partial shade. Tarragon needs a well-draining soil with plenty of room to grow deep roots.

When to harvest

Tarragon should be harvested just prior to the plant flowering to ensure full benefits and flavors.

Parts used

The leaves of the tarragon plant have been used in food preparation and as medicinal remedies.

Medicinal benefits

Tarragon can be used in a variety of ways, including to treat snakebites, insomnia and digestion issues; as an appetite stimulant and a diuretic; and to calm nerves. Using tarragon leaves in a tea can also assist with calming hyperactivity.

Thyme

Thymus vulgaris

Description

Thyme is a perennial that is hardy in zones 5 through 9. It grows to a height of 15 inches with flowers that are pink, purple, or white. It blooms off and on through the summer months.

When to plant

Thyme seeds are easy to grow and can be sown indoors for transplanting in the late spring. The seeds will sprout in about a week. This herb spreads, so space 10 to 12 inches apart.

Sun and soil

Thyme likes full sun or partial shade and light to moderate watering. Soil should be somewhat dry.

When to harvest

Harvest the aerial parts at any time during the summer. They can be hung upside down to dry.

Parts used

Aerial parts, fresh or dried, are used for healing remedies.

Medicinal benefits

Thyme is a good immune system support. It is also recommended for digestive and respiratory concerns. Use as an infusion or tincture.

Valerian

Valeriana officinalis

Description

Valerian has lovely, extremely fragrant flowers that are white with a touch of pink. This plant blooms in late spring. This is a perennial that grows to 4 feet tall.

When to plant

Seeds are easy to start and germinate in seven to 14 days. Start this plant indoors and transplant outdoors in late spring. Seeds can also be sown directly in the garden in early spring.

Sun and soil

Valerian will tolerate full sun, but prefers partial shade and a humus soil. It needs moderate to heavy watering.

When to harvest

The roots of the plant are the parts used. They are harvested in the fall of the first year or the spring of the second year.

Parts used

Roots, either fresh or dried, are used for medicinal purposes.

Medicinal benefits

Valerian is known to be a strong sedative and is also a good pain reliever. Use as a decoction, tincture, or in a capsule.

Vervain

Verbena officinalis

Description

Vervain is a perennial that grows from 1 to 3 feet and is hardy in zones 5 through 9. The plant has slender flower stalks that produce pale purple flowers. It has thin, stiff stems and oblong leaves.

When to plant

This plant grows easily from seeds planted outdoors after all danger of frost passes. This plant will develop roots whenever a stem is on the ground, and this causes it to spread easily. Space plants 12 inches apart in garden bed.

Sun and soil

Vervain likes full sun and well-drained soil. Provide it with low to moderate amounts of water.

When to harvest

Aerial parts are harvested when they are flowering.

Parts used

Flowering aerial parts, fresh or dried, are used.

Medicinal benefits

This plant is used for arthritis pain and sore muscles. Use as a tincture, compress, capsule, or infusion.

Violet

Viola odorata

Description

Violet is a hardy perennial in zones 3 through 7 with sweet-smelling white or purple flowers that bloom from late winter to early spring. The leaves are heart shaped. Violets can be traced back to the 1st century A.D. in Persia, Syria, and Turkey, and the plant is also native to North Africa and Europe. Historically, it has been used as a perfume and medicinal herb. Used as an herb for more than 2,000 years, violet is also central to several folklores and stories. Violet was considered the flower of Aphrodite, the Greek goddess of love, and also of her son, Priapus, the god of the gardens.

When to plant

Violets should be planted in the garden as soon as the last frost is over. Plants should be spaced 12 inches apart and will form a carpet of pretty white and purple flowers throughout the growing season. Violets can easily be started indoors by seed and propagated through root cuttings. Violets will also do well when grown in containers.

Sun and soil

Violets grow best in a shady spot with rich soil. Compost should be added in the spring and fall to encourage growth.

When to harvest

The flowers should be harvested in early spring when they are in full bloom for fresh use or drying. The leaves of the plant can be harvested anytime throughout the growing season. Roots can be dug up in the fall to dry for medicinal uses.

Parts used

The leaves, roots, and flowers of the violet plant can all be used in herbal remedies. The flowers can be crystallized for decoration or used as an addition directly in a salad.

Medicinal benefits

Violet can be used to help brain and nervous conditions like insomnia, anxiety and epilepsy. Additionally, its anti-inflammatory properties can help reduce inflammation and ease the discomforts of rheumatism. Violet can also help ease respiratory conditions like bronchitis, a cold, and coughs and can also reduce mucous and phlegm. Externally, violet is used as a poultice or lotion for sores, acne, eczema, cancerous growths and other skin disorders.

Witch Hazel

Hamamelis virginiana

Description

Hardy in zones 3 through 9, witch hazel is characterized by its bunches of yellow and cream flowers that bloom in late fall through winter. It is a large shrub of several crooked trunks with leaves that turn yellow in the fall. Witch hazel grows 10 to 15 feet high and wide. Native to North America, the forked branches of the plant are commonly used as a tool in divining water and gold. As legend goes, the branches will pull down when near either one of those elements.

When to plant

Witch hazel can be purchased as a shrub at your local nursery or garden center and planted in either the spring or fall. To plant your witch hazel in the garden, dig a hole in the ground that is 2 to 4 inches deeper and wider than the root ball of the plant. Gently put the plant into the hole, add an organic fertilizer or compost, and fill the hole up with soil. Water generously and continue to water well the first year. Once the plant is well-established, it will no longer need watering besides what it naturally receives from rainfall.

Sun and soil

Adaptable to a variety of soil conditions, witch hazel will thrive best in an evenly moist, acidic soil. Witch hazel prefers full sun, but will also tolerate partial shade.

When to harvest

Witch hazel is harvested in the fall and winter seasons.

Parts used

The leaves, branches, stems and flowers of the witch hazel plant are used to make a variety of skin care products and medicinal items like lotions, creams and liquids.

Medicinal benefits

Witch hazel can be used for skin conditions, hemorrhoids, eye injuries, and bleeding; as an antiseptic; and to remedy diaper rash. It has also been used to treat diarrhea, tumors, and dandruff and to decrease the pain and swelling of varicose veins.

Wormwood

Artemisia absinthium

Description

Wormwood is a perennial that stands about 4 feet tall and is hardy in zones 4 through 6. It is especially beautiful in the winter and has clusters of yellowish-green flowers in the summer. The leaves are fern-like and gray-green. A key ingredient in absinthe, wormwood is said to induce clarity of thought, increase one's sense of perception, enhance creativity and infuse inspiration.

When to plant

Sow seeds outdoors in the fall. You can also plant seeds indoors about ten weeks before the last frost and transplant to the garden a week before the last frost. Space wormwood plants 15 inches apart.

Sun and soil

Wormwood prefers full sun, but can tolerate partial shade. It needs well-drained soil and moderate water.

When to harvest

Harvest the branches when the plant is in full bloom. Hang upside down to dry.

Parts used

Aerial parts, fresh or dried, are used for medicinal purposes.

Medicinal benefits

Wormwood is used mainly for gastrointestinal complaints like upset stomach and women's health concerns like PMS. Use as an infusion or tincture.

"The Green Fairy"

Absinthe is an alcoholic drink made from wormwood and a range of other herbs including fennel, anise, lemon balm and hyssop. Actual recipes vary by country and manufacturer. Absinthe first garnered popularity in the late 19th century when it became the preferred drink of writers, intellectuals, artists and poets in France and across other parts of Europe. It later became popular among the general public as well, and its popularity spread as far as New Orleans in America. The nickname "La Fee Verte," which meant the Green Fairy, was given to the drink because of its green color caused by the chlorophyll released from the herbs.

Absinthe was originally served with chilled water. Water was poured into a glass of absinthe over a sugar cube placed on a perforated spoon resting on the top of the glass. This method, known as la louche, is still preferred by all serious absinthe drinkers today. Painters Vincent van Gogh and Henri de Toulouse-Lautrec, along with writers Oscar Wilde and Ernest Hemingway, drank absinthe for its proposed increased clarity of thought, sense of perception and enhanced creativity.

Yarrow

Achillea millefolium

Description

Yarrow is a perennial that grows 1 to 3 feet tall in zones 2 through 8. It has clusters of mainly white to yellow flowers that are flattened. It blooms midsummer through fall. The leaves are fern-like and about 1 inch wide and 6 inches long.

When to plant

Seeds can be planted directly outdoors about a week before the last frost. The plants should be divided in early spring. Space yarrow plants 18 inches apart.

Sun and soil

Yarrow likes full sun but can tolerate partial shade. It needs well-drained, fertile soil and moderate water.

When to harvest

Harvest aerial parts while the plant is in bloom. Hang upside down by the stem to dry by wrapping a string or elastic to the bottom of the stem and attaching the string to a hook or nail.

Parts used

Flowering aerial parts, fresh or dried, should be used.

Medicinal benefits

There are many compounds in yarrow that support its use in healing wounds. Achilletin and achilleine, two chemical compounds found in yarrow, help blood coagulate. It also contains several compounds that have anti-inflammatory and pain-relieving actions, as well as antiseptic properties.

Yerba Mansa

Anemopsis californica

Description

This is an herb that is often substituted for goldenseal. It is a perennial that grows to about 1 foot tall in zones 8 through 9. Yerba mansa's cone-shaped flowers bloom in early summer.

When to plant

Sow seeds indoors in a very warm environment and keep them well-watered. It takes four to six weeks for seeds to sprout. Transplant the seeds outside in early summer and space them 1 foot apart.

Sun and soil

This plant needs full sun and moist soil and should be watered moderately.

When to harvest

Harvest the roots in the fall and dry them by hanging upside down or laying them out on a screen. Dig up the entire plant.

Parts used

The whole plant, fresh or dried, is used.

Medicinal benefits

Yerba mansa can treat inflamed mucous membranes or sore throat. An infusion of the roots can be taken as a diuretic to treat gout. Yerba mansa prevents the buildup of uric acid crystals, which can cause kidney stones. A tea of the roots is used as a douche to staunch bleeding after childbirth. It can also be used in the same way to treat venereal sores. Use as a tea, tincture, infusion, or in a capsule.

These herbs are included as an introduction to herbs and their benefits; however, there are hundreds more herbs available. The next chapters will help you get started with your seeds or plants. You will learn how to ensure good soil conditions, make compost, choose mulch, propagate your favorite plants into new plants and care for your garden.

Chapter 4

GETTING DIRTY

In addition to garden type and location, another key component to creating a medicinal herb garden is the condition of the soil. Soil is important to your herbs because that is where they get the important nutrients they need to grow and remain healthy. Healthy, well-tended soil can be the difference between an herb garden that struggles and one that flourishes. Some things to consider when planting a healing herb garden include the soil's pH level and the benefits of adding fertilizer, compost and mulch to enhance your herbs' growing potential.

Soil

Different plants prefer different types of soil conditions. Some soils are naturally sandy and dry, while others are moist and clay-like. Regardless of the type of soil you start with, by increasing the amount of organic matter in a soil, your herb plants will greatly benefit. Some sources of organic matter that naturally fertilize your soil are grass clippings, leaves, straw, and compost. In addition, you can always add a good store-bought fertilizer. There are many organic fertilizers to choose from, including some that are made with peat moss or worm castings. Earthworms, microorganisms and other soil animals feed on the organic matter in the soil and break it down into nutrients your plants can use. In addition, these soil dwellers improve aeration in the soil by creating little crumb structures or clumps of dirt. The spaces created between the crumbs allow for better airflow to the roots. Soils with crumb structures also retain water better than dense, packed soils.

You will find that herbs are agreeable to almost any type of soil, and most will grow with little trouble in average soil. If your garden plot has average soil or had previously grown grass, adding a couple inches of compost each year should provide enough healthy nutrients for your herbs. If your herb garden site has poor soil or is in a worn-out area, you may want to test your soil to find out what additives you might need to get your garden started.

One main component to the type of soil a plant prefers is its pH level. A soil's pH level refers to the measure of the alkalinity or acidity that is in the soil. Basically, it is the level of lime, or calcium, in your soil. A soil's pH level determines how nutrients and toxic substances will thrive within the soil. The measure of alkalinity is expressed in a range from 0 to 14, where 0 represents extreme acidity and 14 represents extreme alkalinity or extremely basic soil. Most herbs grow well in a pH between 6 and 7, which means the soil is slightly acidic. Before planting your herbs, you should check the pH level of your soil to ensure that your plants will grow to their optimum potential. You can purchase an inexpensive soil test kit at almost any garden center. A typical testing kit provides you with a test tube to which you add your soil and testing solution. If the pH level is not at the optimal level for your herbs, your local garden center will be able to assist you in finding the right additives to adjust it.

When determining the proper pH level for a garden, the current pH level could be either too low or too high for the plants. Because pH is an important factor in how well the plants will thrive, it is important to adjust the pH level of the soil. You can often adjust the pH level yourself.

To increase your pH by 1 point and make your soil more alkaline (less acidic), work the following into the top 4 inches of your garden bed:

- Four ounces of hydrated lime per square yard in sandy soils. A sandy soil is one that is composed of mostly sand and rocks and drains very quickly.

- Eight ounces of hydrated lime per square yard in loamy soils. A loamy soil is a rich, dark soil with lots of organic matter.

- Twelve ounces of hydrated lime per square yard in clay soils. A clay soil is a type of soil that is made up of all to mostly clay.

- Twenty-five ounces of hydrated lime per square yard in peaty soils. Peaty soil has a high concentration of partially decayed vegetable matter and is usually found around moors and wetland forested areas.

To decrease your pH by 1 point and make your soil more acidic, work a fertilizer containing ammonium-N into the top 4 inches of your garden bed. Ideally, any additions to the soil should be worked in a few months prior to planting the herbs. Fertilizers and other amending materials can easily be worked into the soil with a shovel. Once a week, return to the garden area and turn over the soil with the shovel to ensure even application of the fertilizer and other amendments.

Composting

Composting is the process of recycling decaying, organic matter into another material that will improve soil structure and provide nutrients for plants. When a plant dies, microorganisms and insects attack the remains. These organisms help recycle the plant remains into humus. Humus refers to organic matter that reaches a point of stability where it has broken down as far as it can. Humus is a very nutrient-rich soil builder. Compost is used to speed up the breakdown of organic materials. Composting allows you to return nutrients to the soil, which will help your soil retain moisture longer. Compost is also a natural fertilizer that recycles grass and garden clippings, twigs, leaves and kitchen scraps into a usable medium that gives back nutrient-rich organic matter to benefit your garden. In addition, composting your garden is an inexpensive method of improving soil.

Compost can range from a highly managed endeavor to simply allowing your compost heap to sit and decay on its own. How you compost will be determined by the amount of time you want to spend on the task, as well as how much compost you would like to use each season. Space and neighborhood restrictions might also be a factor. For the least amount of time and effort on your part, you might want to simply collect organic material in a freestanding pile. This method will take a long time to decompose, perhaps even a year or two before the material is usable in your garden. If you would like the "pile" to appear more attractive in your yard, you may want to enclose it on three sides with fencing wire or even concrete blocks. Add grass clippings, leaves and kitchen scraps to the pile regularly. If you add kitchen scraps, be sure to cover them with leaves or grass clippings to deter pests and animals. Also avoid adding meat or dairy scraps to your compost as they will smell rotten and attract animals. The size of the pile will shrink as the material breaks down. In about a year, you will have finished compost at the bottom of the pile that you can move and work into your garden beds.

You can also create a pit-style compost area by digging a hole 2 to 3 feet deep. If you choose to use a hole, toss all your compost materials into the pit, and when the it is full, cover it with soil and allow the materials to decompose. The decomposition process cold take up to a year. Once the materials are decomposed, they can be added to your garden. If this method of composting is not fast enough for you, you may want to consider taking a more active role in creating your compost pile.

A more active involvement in the composting process requires more time and energy on your part. The more time you put into your compost pile, the faster it will turn into usable material for your herb garden. When planning your compost area, choose a location in your yard that is level and offers good drainage. You should also make sure the composting area avoids direct sunlight. If your compost pile becomes too dry because of the sun, it will greatly slow down the decomposition process. Find a location that is easy to access and is close to a water source. Avoid putting your compost pile near dog or cat areas because you do not want your pet's urine or feces in your compost, as it will add unwanted pathogens and bacteria. A compost pile should not be located under an overhang because it could limit needed rainfall. You also would not want to place the pile under the eaves of a house that continually drip during or after a heavy rainfall because this will cause the pile to remain too wet. A pile that is too wet will take longer to decompose, as will one that is too dry. Avoid putting your compost pile against anything wooden, like a fence or tree, as the wood will decay along with the compost.

Composting can also be done through either a heap or bin method. If you choose to make a compost heap, find a corner in the garden or yard to start your pile. The piled compost needs to be turned and kept moist on a regular basis, so make sure it is easily accessible. It is a good idea to have a structure when you start your compost because it will keep things tidier. If you live in a suburban neighborhood, you might even want to camouflage your compost pile with tall flowers or a trellis. You can have a compost pile without a supporting structure, but the structure does help keep your composting materials together and is more aesthetically pleasing. You can make a compost structure out of wood, cinder blocks, or even wire. Chicken wire works well, and you can make a round enclosure with it. You can choose to make a square structure with cinder blocks. Make three sides, leaving one side open for access to turn the compost pile.

Instead of creating a compost structure or pile, another option is composting in a bin. In addition to looking nicer, compost bins keep the pile hotter, causing the materials inside to decompose faster. Compost bins also tend to be easier to use; some are even made like a large tumbler with a handle for turning to aerate the compost. Home improvement stores, local garden centers and the Internet are a few resources to find a good composting bin *Refer to Appendix C for suggested resources.*

A variety of things can be incorporated into your compost pile. Soil, manure, table scraps, vegetable and fruit peelings, leaves, small twigs, and annuals from your garden are all things that will help your compost grow. To properly compost, the substances should be a good mixture that bacteria and other microorganisms can easily break down. By using a combination of green matter, like fresh grass clippings, and brown matter, like dried leaves, you will be providing a good mixture of organic matter to your compost pile. A good rule of thumb is to turn the materials with a shovel or fork as you make new additions to the pile to aerate and speed up the decomposition process.

The microbes in the compost pile work best when the compost materials are moist, but not soggy. The microbes need air passages to properly decompose the materials using oxygen. Microbes will also feed on moisture and vegetation like plant leaves and vegetable scraps. This breakdown will create smaller and more soluble molecules. Adding water and turning the pile on a regular basis, usually a couple times a month, will maintain good decomposition. A compost pile should be no smaller than 3 feet by 3 feet by 3 feet and no larger than 5 feet by 5 feet by 5 feet to allow for proper aeration and normal decomposition. A compost pile needs to be physically turned on a regular basis, and a large pile might be too much to manage.

A compost pile can be started any time of the year, and you can build your pile as the materials are available. Fall, however, is a perfect time to begin a compost pile because of the availability of a variety of materials. Fallen leaves, otherwise known as a brown composting material, provide carbon while grass clippings offer nitrogen as a green material. You may also want to invest in a pitchfork to turn your pile. If you have larger materials that you want to incorporate into your compost, such as small tree branches, you may also need pruners or a shredder to cut them up.

Items for a Compost Pile

Brown	Green
Cardboard	Grass clippings
Dead plants	Fruit scraps
Fall leaves (brown and crunchy)	Vegetable scraps
Hay	Coffee grounds
Sawdust	Used tea leaves
Small animal bedding	Plant trimmings
Small wood chips	Green leaves
Straw	Chicken manure

If you choose to become even more active in perfecting your composting skills, you may desire to use a compost thermometer. The temperature of your compost pile indicates the activity that is going on during the decomposition process. You can purchase a compost thermometer to monitor the temperature of your compost at any number of gardening or online retailers. The best decomposing bacteria thrive in a temperature of 110 to 160 degrees. The hotter the temperature of the compost, the faster the compost will break down.

Once you determine where, how and the amount of time you want to devote to your compost pile, it is time to start adding the vital components to create compost. Layering is the recommended and most effective method for starting a compost pile. When the pile becomes active by heating up, you can add materials and mix them in by turning the pile. Compost heaps are layered on the bare ground, unless you choose to start a pile in a composting bin. Watering is important to support the composting process, but be careful not to overwater. Compost should be moist, not soggy. If your compost pile is too dry, the materials will decompose slowly.

If your compost is too wet, it will not allow sufficient aeration for the decomposition process, as the items will be matted down and will smell.

Building your compost pile

The following are the layers you should have in your compost:

Layer 1 — Begin with a layer of twigs, about 2 inches thick, to form air pockets and provide ventilation for other substances. This layer also assists with drainage.

Layer 2 — Add 1 to 2 inches of soil. Be sure to use soil that has not been treated with insecticides, which are unhealthy and decrease the fertility of the soil.

Layer 3 — Add animal manure. Any type of livestock manure is good as long as it is organic and does not contain growth hormones or antibiotics. If the livestock has been treated with any type of medication or growth hormone, these chemicals will find their way into your compost and ultimately into your body as you consume the herbs you applied this compost to. Do not use dog or cat manure as it carries harmful bacteria. If you do not have access to organic livestock manure, you can use fertilizers or starters that will begin the initial heating of your compost pile. There are many compost starters on the market that contain decay-causing microorganisms that speed up or start the composting process. These products can be found at your local garden center. If you are using manure, add a 2-inch layer. If you are using fertilizer, add 1 cup of fertilizer per 25 square feet of compost.

Layer 4 — Organic materials. This layer can be vegetable and fruit peels, crushed egg shells, tea leaves, grass clippings, garden debris, straw, cut up corncobs, coffee grounds, or sod. A bit of cheese, eggs, or milk can go into your compost pile, but large amounts should be avoided. Do not use meat scraps or bones because they smell bad when decaying and will attract animals to your compost pile. There are also many fatty acids in meat that may cause it not to break down completely. Never use plants infected with a bacteria or virus in your compost, or annual or perennial weeds gone to seed, meaning seeds have formed on the plant. The organic materials layer should be 6 to 8 inches deep.

Your compost pile should reach a temperature between 110 to 160 degrees within a couple weeks due to the microbial activity. Once this happens, your pile will begin to settle, which means the materials are breaking down. You can add organic material to your pile at any time, even in the winter. Your compost pile will need to be watered and turned over anytime you add fresh material to the top. It is also ideal to turn your pile when the temperature of the compost goes down. A decreasing temperature means the microbial activity has slowed. A compost pile should be turned every month, but for faster decomposition, you can turn once a week. If you do not add new material, turn and water the pile after it is initially heated. Continue to turn once a month and the compost will be ready in a few months. During the winter months, your compost pile will cool down and activity will stop. If you plan to use it again in the spring, cover the pile with a tarp to prevent water buildup. You can continue to add kitchen scraps all winter without turning your pile. If you live in a tropical climate, you will need to turn your pile throughout the year.

If your compost develops an unpleasant odor, it is often because there is not enough air circulation, which is often a result of overwatering. To remedy this, turn the compost and allow it to dry out. If it smells like ammonia, that is a sign of too much nitrogen. In such a case, you could balance this out by adding more brown material, such as dried leaves. When your compost is dark, crumbly, and smells "earthy," it is ready. This usually takes about three months, depending on the size of your compost pile, the items you add to it, and how often you turn it.

Now that your compost is ready to use, you can incorporate it into your garden soil. If you are planning to till your garden — or turn the soil over — spread a 1- to 2-inch layer of compost on top of the soil and work the compost in with a tiller until it is mixed in. A **tiller** is a type of garden tool with wheels with sharp spikes for plowing or mixing soil. If you do not have a tiller, you can till your garden by hand with a shovel. If you are using compost in an existing garden, shovel compost on top of the soil, use a rake to work it in around the plants and water the mixture thoroughly. You can add compost to your garden at any time, but the best time to use it is when you are preparing the soil for a garden. Organic matter such as leaves, manure, or compost should be added to your garden soil every year to enrich the soil and add back depleted nutrients for your plants to thrive.

CASE STUDY

Carole Miller
Topmost Herb Farm
244 North School Road
Coventry, CT 06238
860-742-8239
www.topmostherbfarm.com
carole@topmostherbfarm.com

Growing both medicinal and culinary herbs, Carole Miller owns and operates Topmost Herb Farm in Coventry, Conn. The herbs on the farm are grown in the "organic way," without commercial fertilizers or pesticides. Instead, organic soil is combined with farm-generated compost and sea and kelp mixtures. Furthermore, herbal plant teas are used for pest and disease control. In addition to offering a variety of organically grown annual and perennial herbs, Miller also lectures to various groups and provides tours of the farm. Her lecture topics include:

- Growing Herbs Organically
- Herbal Appetizers
- Putting the Garden to Bed for the Winter
- The Lore and Legend of Native Medicinal Herbs
- The Herbal Harvest
- Growing Your Own Medicinal Teas
- Ancient Herbs and their Modern Uses
- Making Pesto and Salsa

To begin the process of growing your own medicinal herb garden, Miller recommends that you test your soil. A soil test will provide you with detailed information on which type of nutrients your soil has or does not have. Low levels of nutrients will slow plant growth, whereas too high a level of nutrients can cause imbalances and stress the plants. The soil test will also indicate a pH level, or acidity level of your soil. Some plants prefer an acidic soil, while others will not tolerate an acidic soil at all.

In addition, Miller suggests that gardeners grow organically, especially those plants that are intended for consumption. By making your own compost, for example, you will know exactly what is going into the soil to benefit your plants, and in turn, yourself through the consumption of those plants.

According to Miller, compost can be considered the organic gardener's best ally. She said compost can be made from simple items that many households discard, including dead plants, kitchen vegetable scraps, grass clippings, leaves, newspapers and coffee grounds. After decaying for a few months, these organic materials turn into compost, which returns to the earth the materials that originally came from the earth. It is proven scientifically that organic compost helps combat plant disease and improves the health of the soil by encouraging microbial activity. For additional information on composting, visit **www.topmostherbfarm.com**.

When asked which herb is a good choice for the home gardener, Miller recommends basil due to its ease to grow and use. Basil, according to Miller, makes a great tea and has a wonderful medicinal quality. Basil can calm the nervous system, clear the throat and lungs of congestion, and aid in gastric distress.

In addition to compost, other gardening techniques like using cover crops and mulching can greatly increase the health and productivity of a healing herb garden.

Cover Crops

A cover crop is grown in the garden area during the off-season when your primary crops die off. Cover crops, like compost, help build good-quality and nutrient-rich soil. Cover crops will cut down on weeds, pests and diseases. While cover crops grow, they help protect the soil from wind and water erosion. Grasses and legumes, winter rye, oats, alfalfa and clover are all excellent cover crops. In addition to keeping the soil healthy, these cover crops also provide the opportunity to grow another set of useful plants. A cover crop should be planted in the fall at the end of the growing season. At least four weeks before it is time to plant your herbs for the growing season, till, or turn over, the cover crop into the soil. Let it sit for a couple weeks and then till again. After this step is done, you are ready for planting.

Mulching

Mulching is a key component to the health of your herb garden. In addition to keeping the soil moist, it also limits weeds and pests. Because your herbs deplete the level of nutrients in the soil, mulch will also break down and add those vital nutrients back in.

Mulching can also increase yields, regulate the temperature of the soil, and reduce ground rot to limit crop loss. There are a variety of mulch types available. Ideally, you will want to use organic mulch that will naturally break down to improve drainage and promote soil aeration for your herbs. Organic mulch is made of natural substances that will attract insects and birds. Some examples of organic mulches include peat moss, cocoa shells, bark, compost and even sawdust. Organic mulch will also promote earthworms, which work hard to loosen the soil. You should use organic mulches when growing herbs that will be used for culinary or medicinal purposes to prevent dangerous chemicals from synthetic mulches from leaching into the body. Luckily, organic mulches very often can cost less than manufactured mulches. Homemade compost as a mulch, for example, is free. Your local garden center will be able to assist you with choosing a mulch that is available in your area.

Here is a list of some organic options that may be available in your area:

Type of Mulch	Benefits	Possible Concerns
Pine bark	Available in a variety of sizes Attractive, dark color Good for weed control	May attract termites May float away during heavy rain
Cocoa shells	Beautiful color Smells like chocolate when watered Good for weed control	Toxic to dogs and cats May blow away in wind if not watered
Compost	Cost-effective Adds nutrients to soil Breaks down easily Readily available	Not as attractive as other options
Grass clippings	Readily available Easy to work with High in nitrate	Not attractive Disintegrates quickly
Hay and straw	Improves soil as it decays Easy to walk on Good protective winter mulch	May add weed seeds to soil Not as attractive as other options
Leaves	Easily gathered in yard Decomposes well Adds lots of nutrients	Not attractive May choke plants
Peat moss	Lasts long Light and easy to use	Lowers pH level
Pecan shells	Long-lasting Retains moisture well	Only available in areas where pecans are processed
Pine needles	Great for acid-loving trees, shrubs, and herbs Allows water to penetrate easily Nice natural look	Can be sticky
Wood chips	Available in various sizes Good weed control Decomposes rapidly	May attract termites Depletes nitrogen in soil

Mulch should be added during the spring and fall seasons to ensure proper protective coverage. When adding mulch to your garden, the rule of thumb is to put down a layer that is about 3 to 4 inches deep. Different types of mulch, however, require a slight variation in depth as to not block air circulation, repel moisture, or limit sun exposure. Smaller, finer mulches like sawdust, for example, should only be added in about 1- to 3-inch layers. On the other hand, larger-sized mulches like hay or straw should be somewhere between 3 and 6 inches deep.

Before adding mulch to your herb garden, you need to take a few preliminary steps. First, the garden should be free of weeds. Thoroughly wet the garden, but not so much that the water pools up. As you layer on the mulch, be sure to leave a small space around the base of each plant as to not prevent air circulation. By adding mulch to your herbal healing garden, it will limit the need for a great amount of time spent weeding. It will also keep your plants cool during the hot summer months and protect them better during a freeze and the cycles of wintertime.

Now that you have gotten your hands dirty in soil, compost and mulch, it is time to learn about what can be created from the herbs.

Chapter 5

PROPAGATION AND PLANTING

Purchasing Plants

When starting an herb garden for the first time, you may want to purchase some or all of your herbs as plants instead of growing them from seed or propagating them yourself. This will help you get a feel for growing and caring for your healing herb garden. As you become a more experienced gardener, starting from seed and other propagation methods will become easier and more viable methods for you to try. In addition, many herbs are not propagated from seeds and will need an original mother plant from which to take cuttings for propagation. If you need only one or two plants of a particular variety, it might make more sense to purchase them as single plants. When selecting plants from a nursery or garden center, look for plants that are sturdy and free of disease or pests.

For a solid start in creating a comprehensive and useful healing herb garden, start with the following herbs:

- Aloe
- Comfrey
- Lavender
- Sage

- Lemon Verbena
- Mint
- Rosemary
- Tarragon
- Thyme
- Wormwood

There are four basic methods for propagating plants: growing from seed, taking cuttings from an existing plant, creating a new plant by root or crown division and layering. Propagating your own herbs is an economical and rewarding way to create a garden. The key to successfully propagating your own medicinal herbs is to research and observe the properties and growth habits of the herbal plant you want to propagate. The more information you know about a medicinal plant's specific habits and preferences, the more successful you will be at propagating it.

You can learn more about an individual herb by answering the following questions:

- Where is this herb native to?
- What are the growing conditions of its native location?
- Where would this plant grow if it could choose its own growing location?
- What other types of plants are native to that area?
- Does the herb grow in large clumps? If so, it is most likely propagated through root divisions.
- Do its leaves trail down, or droop? If so, it might be easily propagated through layering.
- Is the herb invasive and takes over other plants?
- What types of roots does the plant have?
- Is the herb an annual, biennial, or perennial?

Some resources for learning about specific herbs and their growing traits are naturalist guidebooks, the Internet and your local garden or horticultural centers. *You can also refer to the detailed herb list in Chapter 3.* Learn as much as you can about the individual plant, its growing habits and where it might grow naturally in the wild to help you identify how you should grow and propagate each individual herb. The propagation method you choose will be based on the individual plant's needs.

Starting from Seeds

Many herbs can easily be started from seed. Starting herbs from seed tends to produce stronger plants, as the plants can more easily adapt to their surroundings. Prior to planting, it is recommended that you refer to the back of a particular herb's seed packet or research its preferences to determine if it should be sown directly into the garden or started indoors. By learning about each individual herb, you will become familiar with those that are best started from seed. Some herbs do not produce viable seeds, have poor germination, and prefer to be started indoors or require to be sown in different seasons.

Spring is the ideal time to sow seeds when the air and soil temperatures are warm, the light levels are higher to provide the necessary sunlight time for proper germination, and the seeds can benefit from spring rains. Some hardy plants like chervil or coriander, however, can also be started in autumn to give them an early start for the following spring. All annuals can be started from seed in the spring.

Some tender herbs need to be started later in the spring when temperatures are warmer. Basil, for example, should be started in late spring to early summer. Biennials like angelica and caraway should be planted in the late summer to early autumn so it can flower the spring or summer of the following year. Perennial herbs can live for a number of years, and not all produce seed. French tarragon, mints and most lavender, for example, are perennial herbs that need to be propagated from another plant, as they do not produce seed. **Vegetative propagation** is the method of creating new plants from cuttings off existing plants.

Starting from seed sounds intimidating, but do not let that deter you. It may be a process of trial and error before you have success, but it is well worth it. There are two choices when starting from seed: purchasing seeds in a packet or saving and cleaning your own seed. Packet seeds are available in a variety of nurseries, garden centers, local growers, or even through catalogs and the Internet. *See Appendix C for some resources.* When purchasing your seeds, keep the following in mind:

- Always purchase from a reputable, well-established seed company that has a good business and product reputation.

- All seeds purchased should be labeled correctly and include both the common and Latin names to ensure exactly which variety you are buying, as there are often several varieties available.

- Look for seeds that are not treated chemically; no fungicides or sprouting agents should have been used on any seeds.

- Ensure that the seeds have not been stored for several years prior to being sold by contacting the seed company directly and asking how old the seeds are.

Saving your own seeds to plant the following growing season is an economical way to enhance your herbal gardens from one growing season to the next. Not only will saving your own seeds save you time and money, but it will also teach you a valuable skill that you will be able to pass on to future generations. Saving seeds is not a difficult task, but you will need to harvest, clean, and store seeds properly to ensure they are viable for the next growing season.

How to Make A Seed Cleaning Screen

To make a small, seed cleaning screen, you will need:

- Four 1" x 3" pieces of untreated and unpainted wood, each 12 inches long
- Eight drywall or decking screws
- A drill

- An old window screen, cheesecloth, or fine fabric netting
- A stapler
- Four 12-inch-long thin wood strips about ¼" x ¾" to hide the staples, or heavy-duty tape
- Wood glue

To make the screen, lay the four pieces of wood on the ground to make a square. Using two drywall screws per corner, attach the pieces of wood together with the drill. Lay the window screen or netting over the wood frame and staple around the square, pulling the screen taught as you go. Use the tape or glue the thin wood strips along the staple line to hide the staples.

Here is a simple three-step seed-saving process:

1. Harvest — The ideal time to harvest seeds from your garden is when the seeds are fully ripe. The seeds should be fully formed, dry, and plump looking. Usually, the seed will have turned from a greenish color to something a little different from its original color like white, black, tan, maroon, brown, or even speckled. You can either pick the seeds by hand or use a pair of good garden shears. Use a dry container to gather your seeds, such as a paper bag or tightly woven basket. To discourage the growth of mold on your seeds, do not store them in an airtight plastic storage container.

2. Clean — When you gather your seeds, you need to clean them for storage. Use a shallow cardboard box or some newspaper spread out on a table to begin the process. Because seeds are usually contained within a protective barrier, husk, or shell, you will need to gently dislodge the seed from its house. Many garden centers and nurseries sell specific seed-cleaning screens, but you can make your own by using a tea strainer, fabric netting, cheesecloth, or even an old window screen. Place the seeds on your screen and gently shake back and forth to remove the chaff

from the seeds. The **chaff** refers to the remaining pieces of the seed's house that cling to the seed. Very often, you will not be able to remove all of the chaff from the seed and some of it will remain. This will not hinder the sowing process.

3. Store — After you harvest and clean the seeds, you need to find a good place to store them before the next growing season. A plain paper envelope will work. To keep track of your seeds, it will be helpful to label the envelopes as follows:

    • NAME: name of the plant (common and Latin for proper identification)

    • DATE: date seeds were harvested

    • LOCATION: location where seeds were harvested

The envelopes should then be placed in a plastic zip-top bag and stored in the freezer. Most seeds will remain viable this way for three to seven years, depending on the seed. Tropical seeds, however, should not be stored in the freezer. Instead, store them in a dry location at room temperature. For all seeds, avoid excess heat.

After you purchase or gather the seeds for your herb garden, you need to prepare your seeds before you sow them. In nature, plant seeds often go through a variety of conditions before they settle into their final resting place to germinate. They are often torn from their plants by forceful winds or by birds, causing damage to their outer shells. In other cases, they must go through a period of dormancy before they are ready to germinate again. Some hard-coated seeds like clovers need to go through a scarification process to replicate the conditions they experience in nature. It is important to rub a seed that requires scarification with fine sandpaper or a nail file to break up its outer coating to allow moisture to penetrate before the seed can germinate. Other herbs like monkshood, sweet woodruff, or hawthorn need to go through vernalization or stratification. Some seeds need to experience periods of wetness like those that occur in nature through snow cover. By soaking a seed, it will soften the outer layer and allow for easier germination. To soak seeds, place them in a small bowl and pour warm to hot water over them. Allow them to soak overnight before planting them. The back of the seed packets will be able to provide you with any special requirements for starting the seeds.

When your seeds are ready for germination, they can be started either indoors in seed trays or sown directly into your outdoor gardens. Although either method will work just fine, seeds started under controlled conditions in seed trays tend to have a higher success rate.

Sowing seeds indoors

Supplies for starting your own herbs from seed can be purchased at any number of local nurseries, garden stores, home improvement stores, catalogs, or on the Internet. To start your seeds in a seed tray, you will need:

- Divided seed trays, which are plastic trays with divided sections and clear domes or covers

- Good, porous soil mix that clearly indicates potting soil on the bag

- Seeds

- Labels

- Mister or spray bottle

- Sunny location

- 3-inch pots

First, select a container to plant your seeds in. Plastic seed trays, peat pots, newspaper pots and even egg cartons can be used to start seeds. The benefit of using a biodegradable container, like peat pots or newspaper pots, is that both the seed and the pot can be planted directly into the garden and will slowly decompose over time. This does not disturb the root base of your new seedling, and the shock from transport is greatly reduced. On the other hand, most gardeners prefer plastic seed trays or pots as they retain moisture better.

Next, consider your planting soil. Most seeds germinate best in a porous soil medium. Various soil types can include sand, perlite (a volcanic product), peat moss from swamps, crushed stones, sterilized topsoil, or even sphagnum moss, which comes from bogs. These soil types are readily available at your local gardening center or home improvement store. Most good-quality potting mixes include a combination of soil mediums to allow for proper germination and growth. Your local garden center will be able to assist you in finding a good potting soil for starting your herb seeds.

Sowing seeds in trays

1. Fill the seed tray three quarters of the way full with your potting soil.

2. Water the soil.

3. Poke holes with your finger about ½ inch deep into the compartments of the tray.

4. Add your seeds, two to four seeds per compartment.

5. Cover the seeds with soil and water again; be careful not to bury the seeds too deeply, especially smaller seeds, as they will not get the proper amount of light needed to germinate.

6. Label your compartments.

7. Cover the tray with a plastic dome.

8. Place the tray in a warm, sunny location.

9. Continue to keep the seeds moist.

10. Once the small green seedlings emerge from the seed, remove the cover and place them in a well-lit place, but out of direct sunlight.

11. Continue to keep seeds moist.

12. Thin the seedlings to keep one or two strong plants per compartment by removing extra seedlings.

When the seeds germinate and produce several leaves, they are ready to be transplanted into small, 3-inch pots. This will allow the plant to develop a stronger root system before going into the garden. Fill the 3-inch pots with potting soil and make a well with your finger into the soil to the depth of your seedling. To transplant the seedlings to the 3-inch pots, gently remove the plant from its compartment and place into the well in the soil of the pot. Fill the well with soil to support the seedling. Be very careful not to damage the stem or roots while you are moving it from the compartment to the larger individual pot. Let the seedlings grow for a few more weeks until they are larger in size and sturdier in appearance before moving them to their permanent location. Through this entire process, it is important to keep the seeds and seedlings moist, but not wet enough where they will grow fungus. The soil around the seedlings should be damp to the touch, but not puddle. An efficient method that will decrease possible damage to the roots and plant is to use biodegradable seed compartment trays and pots. Rather than having to remove the entire plant from its location, you will be able to transplant the entire pot directly into the soil.

Sowing seeds outdoors

Many herbal seeds can be sown outdoors directly into the garden, which decreases the chance of damaging the seeds through transplanting them from a pot. Coriander, chervil and dill, for example, do not respond well to being transplanted and are best sown directly into the garden. Due to unexpected weather conditions and the threat of wild animals, seeds sown directly outdoors have a higher failure rate than those sown indoors. Sowing seeds directly outdoors, however, saves time and energy. In addition, plants sown directly outdoors are often sturdier.

To sow seeds directly outdoors in your herbal garden:

1. Do not start seeds too early in the spring, as the ground has not thoroughly warmed up yet.

2. Weed the area and rake it to a level surface.

3. Create shallow impressions in the ground, about 1 inch wide by 1 inch deep, where you want your herbs planted.

4. Place three herb seeds into each impression and cover with a thin ¼-inch layer of soil. Pat down lightly.

5. Mark the area with an identification tag to ensure you remember where you sowed the seeds. You can purchase tags at your local garden center or make them by using a waterproof marker to write the name of the herb on a rock.

6. Water thoroughly, and keep the area moist until seedlings emerge.

7. Thin seedlings to the distance suggested on the seed packet.

For the best results when starting herbs from seed, research what particular seeds need. If a seed requires stratification, for example, you need to recreate the freeze and thaw cycle. Other seeds need to be soaked to germinate more easily. By following a specific herb's requirements, you will have greater success at starting herbs from seed for your healing garden. Healing herbs that do well started from seed can be found in the following list.

Healing Herbs Easily Started from Seed

Alfalfa	Cilantro	Mullein
Angelica	Corn	Motherwort
Anise hyssop	Dandelion	Oregano
Astragalus	Dill	Nasturtium
Basil	Echinacea	Nettle
Black-eyed Susan	Elecampane	Passionflower
Boneset	Fennel	Plantain
Borage	Feverfew	Red clover
Calendula	Flaxseed	Sheep sorrel
California poppy	Hyssop	Shepherd's purse
Chamomile	Lavender	Skullcap
Catnip	Lemon balm	Thyme
Cayenne	Lemongrass	Valerian
Celery	Lovage	Vervain
Chicory	Marshmallow	Wormwood
Chrysanthemum	Milk thistle	

CASE STUDY

Jen Syme
Jen's Bouquets, a division of
Syme's Flower Farm
Broad Brook, CT
860-623-5925
symemums@cox.net

Syme's Flower Farm in Broad Brook, Conn., is a family owned and operated business that grows and sells 15 different varieties of herbs, many different perennials, and vegetable plants for spring sales. The family business also grows and sells flower bouquets and annual patio pots for summer sales and more than 3,000 fall flowering mums for late summer and early fall sales. In addition to two self-service roadside stands of cut flowers and other items, they also sell through a cut flower subscription program and at local farmers markets. One hundred percent of the herbs sold by the family are grown directly from seed.

Jen Syme has a degree in horticulture from the University of Connecticut College of Agriculture and Natural Resources. She grows from seed primarily because of the economics of growing. According to Syme, "Seeds are generally inexpensive to purchase and readily available. I can tailor my planting time to my expected sales date and time schedule. If I have poor germination, I am not out a whole lot of money. Nothing is more satisfying than to know that you started with a tiny seed, coaxed it along through the seedling stage, and produced a mature, saleable, viable plant. Herb plugs — small herb plants already started — are available to buy, but I like being able to control when and how much I plant."

According to Syme, one of the easiest herbs to grow from seed is any variety of basil. Basil has visible germination within five to seven days — sometimes sooner — and is a very fast-growing, popular culinary herb. Basil is "easily one of my best sellers year after year," she said. "Who can resist the smell of basil?" On the other hand, one of the most challenging herbs to grow is rosemary because "it takes a long time to germinate, sometimes as long as three weeks, and has a history of low germination rates, even with primed seed. Seedlings can be fussy, especially when it comes to moisture."

Syme offers the following advice to starting herbs from seed:

- Always start with clean containers. If you are planting into previously used containers, make sure that you clean them well with a bleach solution to alleviate any problems later on.

- Pay attention to the germination information. The back of a seed packet holds a wealth of information. Some seeds need to be chilled first and some need to be covered to create darkness to germinate. Some seeds will germinate in a few days given the correct requirements; others can take weeks. They all have different requirements.

- Pay attention to how early you should plant your seeds in the spring. Most seed packets/companies will indicate the number of weeks a plant should be started indoors prior to moving them outdoors for the growing season.

- If you do not have a greenhouse, heat mats will speed up the germination process. Heat mats are thermostat-controlled mats that the seedling pots sit on top of to warm the soil.

- Have fun growing herbs from seed! Experiment a little. Try something new. It's no big deal if a certain variety doesn't work out; try something else. It is fun to grow the more common herbs, but don't be afraid to try new varieties.

Creating New Plants from Cuttings

Some herb plants do not produce seed, and therefore need to be propagated through different methods. Comfrey, as an example, must be started from cuttings, as it does not produce seed. Certain herbs like spearmint have high amounts of volatile, or essential, oils that will grow less potent when started from seed. Cuttings can be taken from either the stem or root of an existing plant. Rosemary, for example, is best propagated from stem cuttings. Herbs with creeping roots like mint or those with taproots like horseradish are best propagated from the roots.

Cuttings from stems

Taking cuttings from stems during the growing season is an excellent way to propagate new plants. A **softwood cutting** refers to the process of taking cuttings from soft, new growth on a plant in the spring to early summer. Taking cuttings from a plant in mid- to late summer is referred to as a **semi-ripe cutting**. Taking cuttings from fully mature wood of the plant's stem base in mid- to late autumn is known as a **hardwood cutting**. Hardwood cuttings tend to be slow to root — up to 12 months — and oftentimes have to be kept in a cold frame for protection over winter. A cold frame is an unheated outdoor structure consisting of a wooden or concrete framed base with a glass or plastic top. For most healing herbs, you will use either softwood or semi-ripe cuttings.

To create new plants from stem cuttings, you need:

- Plants
- Sharp knife or pruners
- Shady spot
- Rooting hormone, which can be purchased at a garden center or online
- Potting soil medium
- Pencil or stick to make holes
- Small pots
- Plastic dome or bag

When starting plants from stem cuttings, collect only a small amount — two to three pieces — at a time and keep them in the shade to minimize drying out. Before taking your cuttings, fill your pot three-quarters full with potting soil, water the soil and poke one hole per cutting in the soil with a pencil or stick. For the cuttings, choose non-flowering, strong stems with lots of leaves. Using your knife or pruners, cut a 1-inch to 4-inch piece just below a leaf joint. Remove all but the top two sets of leaves from the cutting. Dip the cuttings into the rooting hormone and place them into the holes made by the pencil. Cover with a plastic dome or plastic bag that is secured to the bottom of your pot. This will ensure the proper humidity for the cutting to take and begin to grow roots. Once the cutting is rooted, which should take two to four weeks, repot into new soil with compost and harden them off before planting them outdoors. To harden your new plants off, keep them in a sunny, warm room and slowly transition them outdoors before planting them outside. When creating stem cuttings, remember to take only one-third to one-half of the tender growth available, as more than that can stress and damage the mother plant.

Cuttings from roots

Root cuttings are the ideal method for propagating creeping herbs like oregano and bergamot. To create cuttings from roots, you need:

- Plants
- Garden fork
- Pruners
- Seed tray
- Good potting soil

Carefully dig up a root from a mature plant you would like to make cuttings from. Gently shake off the soil from around the root. Cut the root into 1-inch to 2-inch pieces. Ideally, you should try to cut the root where there is a bud, which looks like a bump, from which a new plant can grow. Fill a seed tray with potting soil and lay the pieces of root on the surface of the dirt. Press the roots into the soil slightly and cover with a thin layer of soil. Water and leave in a shady location. Leave uncovered, but continue to keep the soil moist. Once there are plenty of leaves coming through the top of the soil, divide the new plants and place them in larger pots or directly into the garden.

Some Healing Herbs to Start from Cuttings

Herb Name	Method of Cutting
Boneset	Softwood in Spring
Chrysanthemum	Stem
Elder	Hardwood
Hibiscus	Stem
Mint	Stem or Root
Hops	Root
Oregano	Stem
Rosemary	Stem
Stevia	Stem
Thyme	Root
Vervain	Stem
Yerba Mansa	Root

Root Division

Herbs with a branching root system that grows laterally under the surface, also referred to as **rhizomatous plants**, are best propagated through root division. **Root division** is simply the process of separating plants at the root base to create more than one plant. Root divisions are ideally done in early spring or early fall, causing less stress on the plant.

To propagate through root division:

- Carefully dig up a mature plant that you want to divide into more than one plant.

- Gently remove the soil from around the roots and lay the plant on its side.

- Using your hands, gently pull the plant apart at the roots by dividing the root clump into several pieces.

- Replant each division piece into the ground.

- Cut off some of the top growth, above the soil, to promote root growth.

- Remember to keep the plants well watered.

Some healing herbs to start from root division

- Chamomile
- Chives
- Chrysanthemum
- Comfrey
- Goldenseal
- Gotu kola

- Lemon balm
- Lovage
- Oregano
- Passionflower
- Yarrow

Layering

Layering is a useful method of propagation for shrubby herbs with runners or offshoots. Runners and offshoots are long stems that shoot out and grow from the mother plant. Bay, rosemary and sage, for example, are often well propagated through layering. Layering encourages a branch to create roots by being bent down into the soil. An advantage to layering is that it does not cause injury to the existing plant or to the new plant growth. It does, however, take longer than starting new plants through the cutting method.

Layering works by creating new roots on a side stem while still attached to the parent plant. In the case of thyme, for instance, mound layering is an effective propagation method and can be achieved by piling loam over lower leafless stems while leaving the crown of the plant exposed. This will stimulate new roots to develop at the base where they can be separated and planted in a different location. Ideally, layering should be done in the spring prior to the buds opening up on your plant.

To create a new herb through layering:

- Choose a long, strong branch that is still flexible and bends easily.
- Trim the lower leaves.
- Bend the branch down to the ground.
- Add some peat moss or sand where the branch meets the ground.
- Fasten the branch down with a staple, peg, or even a heavy rock.
- Water regularly.

After several months, usually the following spring, the branch will have produced sufficient roots to be replanted on its own. To remove the new plant, carefully dig it up and cut it just below the new roots from the mother plant. It is now ready to plant in its new home.

Some healing herbs to start from layering include:

- Catnip
- Lavender
- Lemon balm
- Rosemary
- Sage
- Thyme

Crown Propagation

Herbaceous plants — non-woody plants with soft green stems — can be propagated through crown division. Crown division is a method by which a clumping plant is dug up, divided into smaller clumps and replanted. The ideal time for doing crown division, or propagation, is in the fall just after the plant dies back.

To propagate through crown division:

- Carefully dig up the plant.
- Brush away the dirt from the plant.
- Divide the **crown**, the very top that sticks out of the soil, of the plant into several pieces. You may need to use a spade or sharp knife.
- Replant the crowns into new locations.

Healing herbs to start from crown propagation include:

- Chamomile
- Garlic
- Hyssop
- Mugwort
- Onion

Propagating your own plants through a variety of methods can be an economical and enjoyable way to create additional herbs for your gardens year after year. Keep notes in your binder as you go through the process of starting from seed, taking cuttings, dividing and layering to keep track of your results with various methods. This will come in handy from year to year as your garden matures and grows.

Regardless of whether you start your herbs from seed, use another propagation method, purchase them from a nursery as plants, or use a combination of all three, you will cultivate a garden that will provide you with enjoyment and satisfaction for years to come.

Chapter 6

GARDEN CARE

Herbs are plants that, once established, should not require more than the standard plant care of thinning, watering, weeding, dividing, pest control and winterizing. Regular seasonal care and maintenance will keep your medicinal herb garden looking and performing its best. Rather than viewing garden care as a chore that must be done, look at it from the perspective of a healing process. In caring for your medicinal plants, you are creating a garden that will heal and nourish body and soul.

Thinning the seedlings in your healing garden, for example, will help plants to reach their full growing potential. If your herbs are overcrowded, they will not get enough sunlight or nutrients to remain healthy. Ideally, you need to thin seedlings, or remove any that are too close together, once they are well established. Your seedlings are ready to be thinned to the proper spacing distance once they have one or two sets of leaves. The best way to thin seedlings in your garden is to pull any "extra" plants, which occur when the seedlings are too close together. To determine how far apart your individual healing herbs should be spaced, research the growing size of the particular herb.

Keeping paths, beds and walkways organized and free of weeds will enhance the look of your garden. For a formal herb garden, you may want to keep plants clipped and trimmed. Plants can be clipped by snipping off any growth that sticks up beyond the desired shape. Most herbs only require cutting twice a year. In most cases, many herbs, if left to themselves, will become overgrown and untidy looking. Taking small clippings regularly throughout the growing season should keep your plants looking neat. Cutting your plants down to a few inches above the ground level will promote growth. Pest and weed control will also keep your plants healthy and viable.

Weed Control

Weeds can be a big problem in any garden if they are allowed to get out of control. Weeds are simply plants you do not want growing where they decided to put down roots. Because manufactured chemicals can be harmful to your herbs and are not safe for use on plants that are used as foods and medicines, the best solution for weed control is digging them up. The most effective method to getting rid of weeds organically is by pulling them out of the ground before they go to seed. Weeding after a good rain makes it easier to pull them up out of the ground. Weeding your herb garden will destroy competition for nutrients in the garden and allow for plenty of room for your herbs to grow and thrive. Weeding will also cut down on diseases and insects in your garden.

Here are some weeding tips:

- Weed early and often during the first part of the season.
- Try to get weeds up with as little digging as possible as to not disturb the roots of the other plants.
- Once a garden is prepared, planted and weeded, try to avoid turning the dirt over, as it can expose additional buried weed seed to sunlight and promote growth of additional weeds.
- Mulch heavily to help cut down on weed growth.

After living with your herb garden for a few years, you will discover that weeds tend to come up in batches. The first set of weeds will appear in spring. These weeds are normally winter annuals that germinated the previous fall. If they are allowed to go to seed, the will come up again later in the spring. Then, just as you think those weeds are gone, the frost-sensitive, heat-loving weeds of summer will appear. The best form of weed control is to try and pull weeds up as soon as they appear so they do not have the opportunity to re-seed themselves.

Caring for Your Garden by Season

To keep your medicinal herb garden performing at its peak, you will want to keep it maintained by completing certain seasonal chores. You may want to make notes in your binder about which chores to perform and when as a guide to help you maintain your garden and keep it at optimal health.

Spring

Spring is the ideal time to begin planting your garden to enjoy a summer of healthy and vital plants. Spring is a good opportunity to make any adjustments to the soil, create new beds and start seeds indoors. Spring is the season during which gardens normally get the most natural moisture in the form of rainfall. Take advantage of the added moisture and add plenty of organic matter that will hold moisture for the long summer days ahead. Add compost to your beds and work it into the soil.

Spring is also a good time to add a mulch cover to help prevent weeds from growing. When adding new plants to the garden, consider their final growth size and spacing to ensure there is plenty of room for growth. Your early spring garden may appear sparse when you first plant it, but it will be full during the summer months as the herbs fill out. This is also a good time to cut back certain herbs and remove last year's dead growth. Removing the previous year's growth will promote new development for the season. Spring is also a good time to take cuttings to create new plants. In your gardening binder, you can make notes of which plants you planted, where they were planted and perhaps which ones came back from the previous season.

Summer

Summer brings with it hot days and warm nights. Summer is the time to take great care in watering your herb garden to promote growth. Watering is best done first thing in the morning before the heat of midday sun. If you water during midday sun, from about 11 a.m. to 3 p.m., you run the risk of burning your plants. As the sun burns the water off, it can scorch the leaves, flowers and stems of your plants. If you water in the evening, your herbs may develop fungi as they do not get enough sun to sufficiently dry out.

Summer is also a good time to add fertilizer to your garden for an extra boost to make it through the remainder of the growing season. By adding a compost tea, which is created by brewing compost in water, or even a fish emulsion, you can significantly increase your herb production. During summer, you also want to pinch your herbs back by snipping off the tops and take regular cuttings to promote growth. This is also a good time to work on your compost pile and take care of any pests or diseases that may be distressing your plants by removing affected leaves and applying an insecticidal soap.

Compost Tea

To make a compost tea for your medicinal herb garden, you will need:

- Plastic container, pail, barrel, or watering can
- Small to medium cloth bag
- Fresh compost, about 1 gallon
- Water, 5 gallons

Gather the compost in the cloth bag and steep in a container filled with water. Allow to brew for three days, stirring occasionally. The water will turn a brown color. After three days, remove the cotton bag and add its contents back to the compost pile. The liquid, which is the compost tea, is now ready to be added to the garden.

Because summertime is also when many people go away on vacation, you may want to set up a plan to ensure that your herbs receive water while you are away. Not getting the proper amount of water during the hot summer months could badly damage your herbs and render them useless for harvesting. Start by thoroughly watering your plants right before departing, and make arrangements to have your herb gardens watered by a trusted neighbor or friend. Investing in automatic timers and soaker watering hoses, which have a series of small holes up and down the length of the hose, would also benefit your garden.

During the summer season, you may also want to get out your camera and take pictures of your herbs at their peak. By adding pictures to your binder, you will be able to enjoy the beauty of your garden throughout the long winter months. Add the pictures to your binder with notes on how well they grew in their current conditions. Did they get the proper amount of water and sun where you planted them? If not, make plans on where you might want to grow that particular herb the following season. You may also want to jot down how much you were able to harvest and use from a particular herb to determine if you need to grow more or less the following season.

Fall

Garden maintenance in the fall is a very important step to maintain a healthy herb garden from year to year. The first step in fall garden maintenance is to get organized and make a list of what needs to be done. Determine which herbs to cut back, which ones to bring indoors in the winter and which ones to add to the compost pile; annual herbs, as well as the clippings made from cutting back your perennial herbs, can be added to the compost pile. Take stock and make a note of any herbs you may want to move for the next growing season. Sometimes you may want to move an herb that has crowded out other plants in the garden or has not grown to its full potential in its current location. The most efficient way to start organizing fall clean up is by going through your gardens to determine what to do with your annual, container and perennial herbs.

The Harvest Moon

The full moon that appears closest to the fall equinox in late September to early October is traditionally referred to as the harvest moon. The harvest moon appears bigger, brighter and more colorful, often with a spectacular reddish-orange hue, than the other moons in the lunar cycle. It is named the harvest moon as it allows more light and, subsequently, extra work time for farmers to gather the bounty of the fall crops.

With annual herbs, you can either leave them in the ground until you are ready to replant in the spring, or you can pull up any that are beginning to yellow and add them to your compost pile. Make notes in your binder of which annual herbs grew best and those that did not grow well so you have a good starting point for planning next year's garden. For annuals grown in containers, you can add the plant, complete with its roots and soil, to your compost pile.

For tender perennial herbs grown in containers, you may want to move them indoors to a protected area before winter arrives. An unheated garage or basement works well for this. To prepare these herbs to move indoors, allow the containers to dry out, but not to become completely parched. The reason for doing this is to prohibit growth during the winter season. By moving them into a more protected area, your tender perennials will be able to go through a natural dormancy period without experiencing damage from the harsh weather conditions of winter.

For any root-bound invasive perennials that you grew in pots, either add them to your compost pile or divide them into smaller plants to repot. Invasive perennial herbs are subject to becoming root-bound as they grow an excessive amount during the growing season and quickly outgrow their pots. A root-bound plant grown in a container will not grow well year after year in the same container because it is difficult to supply the proper amount of water and nutrients to combat the stress caused by being grown in a contained pot.

Contrary to common thought, fall is not the time to cut off dead growth from perennial herbs. The material left on your herbs until spring can provide food for birds and other creatures throughout the winter. For any spreading herbs that outgrew their boundaries, however, you may want to cut these back to the ground so they can start small again come spring. For any plants that you wish to transplant in the spring, you may want to mark them now to make locating them in the spring easier. Fall is also the time to consider growing a cover crop. *Refer to Chapter 4 for tips on cover crops.*

Winter

A valuable facet of herb gardening is winterizing your perennial herb plants so that they can survive the harsh winter months. By properly **winterizing** — preparing your plants to survive throughout the winter — you will ensure a bounty of useful herb plants come spring and summer. Through the process of preparing your garden for winter, remember that nature has its own way of winterizing itself. As the season approaches, the growth of your plants slows down, and many of the herbs lose their leaves and look as if they are withering and dying. It may appear as if your perennial herb is dead, but, in fact, it is only going into its dormant stage to survive the winter.

Less hardy plants, like rosemary and oregano, may not survive the winter chill. You can either take a chance and see if they return the following season, or dig them up, place them in pots and let them spend the winter inside. You may need to experiment with the hardiness levels of different plants in your area to determine which ones should come inside and which can be left outdoors. Consult the specific herb's hardiness level for your area, or ask your local garden center or your neighbors to find out what they have the best luck with in your area.

As for fertilizing your garden, all fertilization should stop by early August, as you will not want any new growth happening during the fall season.

Any tender new growth that occurs during the fall will be damaged by the winter frost. Trimming, likewise, should also be avoided, as it will stimulate new growth and tax the herb's stored energy. As winter approaches, keep your plants fairly dry. As winter comes closer, watering will pull the heat away from your plant and may also cause freezing. Water freezing around the base of your plants may crack their roots and cause damage.

To thoroughly protect your garden and ensure that your perennial herbs will withstand the harsh winter months, pay particular attention to mulching your herb gardens. In all but the very warmest of climates (zones 10 and 11), perennial herbs should be well mulched during the winter. The ideal time to mulch is when the plants are securely dormant and the top ½ inch to 1 inch of the ground is frozen. If in doubt about the proper timing, before mulching, wait until nighttime temperatures reach a level in the 20s and daytime temperatures have been at the freezing mark for three to four days in a row. Materials that make good winter mulches include shredded leaves, hay and straw. For the best coverage, apply a layer of mulch about 6 inches deep over the bed where the plant is. In addition to protecting the plant throughout the winter, the mulch will also break down and provide nutrients to the soil around your plants. You will have to remember in the very early spring to pull the mulch away from the crown, or very top, of your plants to promote spring growth. Be prepared to cover tender new growth in the spring if there is a late frost.

Wind and heavy snowfall can also cause damage to your herbal healing garden during the long winter months. To eliminate damage that a harsh winter may cause, you may want to protect your herb plants further with burlap shields strung between wooden posts. Start by putting wooden posts in the ground around your plants in either a rectangular or triangular pattern. Staple burlap to the top of the posts to make a tent to protect the plants. The burlap will also decrease the wind's drying effect on your plants.

Early winter is also the best time to clean and store your gardening tools. To protect your metal shovels, rakes and garden clippers from rust, dip them in a pail that contains sand mixed with mineral oil to remove rust and protect them over the winter. Hang tools to store. Thoroughly clean any pots that you used over the summer. Wash your pots with hot, soapy water, and allow them to dry before storing them in a protected area like a shed or garage for the winter. You can also clean and disinfect your pots, especially if a plant in one of them had carried a disease, by washing them in 9 parts water to 1 part bleach. Following the bleach cleaning, the pot should be washed again to remove any residue left by the bleach. To clean bleach residue, wash in 9 parts water to 1 part vinegar. If you leave your ceramic pots outside during the winter months, they may crack due to the freezing and thawing cycles.

Companion Planting to Prevent Pest Problems

Because many pests are repelled by the strong scent of herbs, you will not find many pests invading your healing garden. In fact, you should plant certain herbs as companion plants to help keep pests away. Herb gardens that contain a variety of plants will naturally repel most pests.

For the best pest and disease protection in your healing garden, implement the following tips:

- Mix different herbs together in one bed.

- Grow annual herbs in a different section of the bed every year.

- Every four years, transplant the perennials to a different location.

- Use compost and organic matter to encourage beneficial organisms.

- Weed, feed, water, mulch and keep the areas surrounding your plants free of debris to maintain a healthy garden with limited places for pests to hide.

- Learn to recognize pests beneficial to your garden so that you do not accidently get rid of the ones that help.

Learning to identify the most common pests in your herb garden is your biggest defense in managing insects in your healing herb garden. Some of the most common offensive bugs are listed below:

Pest	Description	Herbs Affected	Solution
Aphid	1/12-1/5" oval shaped; can be red, white, green, black, or yellowish in color	Caraway, chervil, oregano, parsley, nasturtium	Squash by hand Insecticidal soap Strong spray of water
Beetle	¼-1" oval shaped with a hard shell; come in a variety of colors	Eats the stems and leaves of a variety of herbs. Japanese beetles particularly like basil.	Insecticidal soaps Removing by hand
Carrot weevil	1/5" flat bug; brownish with darker spots	Parsley	Squash by hand Crop rotation
Cutworm	1-2" slimy looking gray or brown caterpillar	Prefers most seedlings	Place cardboard collars on seedlings or insert toothpicks around stem to block from plant
Earwig	¼" long, narrow brown semi-hard shelled	Angelica	Handpick from plants Avoid wood mulches
Leaf miner	1/10", not visible to the eye, but you will see tunnels they create in your plant's leaves	Angelica, lovage, nasturtium, oregano, sorrel	Remove and destroy infected leaves
Mealy bug	1/10-¼" flat, grayish white oval-shaped bug with many legs	Rosemary	Hard spray of water Insecticidal soap
Parsley worm	2" swallowtail butterfly larvae: greenish-yellow, black-striped caterpillar	Parsley	Handpicking
Slugs	3" slimy soft-bodied; gray, brown or black	Can affect a variety of herbs including basil, calendula, sage and violet	Handpicking Insecticidal soaps Put beer traps by placing shallow containers with about ½" of beer at base of plants

Pest	Description	Herbs Affected	Solution
Spider Mite	1/50" miniature spider-like red, green, or yellow bug	Angelica, lemon verbena, mint, oregano, rosemary, sage, thyme	Insecticidal soaps
Whitefly	1/12" triangular white insect	Lemon verbena, rosemary	Insecticidal soaps

While trying to rid your garden of pests, you may want to learn to recognize some beneficial gardening insects like lacewing, syrphid fly, lady beetle, predatory mite and tachnid flies that feed on harmful garden pests.

You can also put your herb garden to good use by planting herbs that will help repel pests in your other gardens and around your home.

Pest	Repelling Herb
Ants	Tansy, wormwood
Aphids	Chives, cilantro, fennel, peppermint, spearmint
Cabbage loopers	Anise hyssop, chives, nasturtiums, tansy, sage
Carrot rust flies	Chives, rosemary, sage, wormwood
Codling moths	Wormwood
Colorado potato beetles	Catnip, cilantro, nasturtiums, tansy
Cucumber beetles	Catnip, nasturtiums, rue
Flea beetles	Rue, tansy, wormwood
Imported cabbage moths	Anise hyssop, chives, dill, sage, wormwood
Japanese beetles	Catnip, chives, garlic, tansy
Mexican bean beetles	Rosemary, summer and winter savory
Slugs and snails	Fennel, garlic, rosemary
Spider mites	Cilantro
Squash bugs	Catnip, nasturtiums, tansy
Tomato horn thorns	Borage, dill, basil
Whiteflies	Nasturtiums, thyme, wormwood

Disease Control

Diseases in a home herb garden are a rare occurrence, but they can happen. Herbs are some of the hardiest, disease- and pest-resistant plants around. They have very few problems and naturally repel pests. Additionally, herbs like rosemary and sage prefer growing conditions that most plants would not survive in. Appropriate spacing and weeding will keep humidity levels down in your garden and help prevent disease. A good, nutrient-rich soil will strengthen plants, increasing their ability to tolerate disease. Air movement and watering patterns will affect how susceptible your herbs are to disease. If your plant gets a disease, the first step is to be able to properly identify it so you can treat it effectively. Some diseases are localized and can be remedied by plucking off the affected leaves. To avoid spreading fungal spores to healthy plants, always wash your hands, clothes and tools thoroughly after handling diseased plants.

Common diseases that may affect your herb plants include the following:

Disease	Herbs Bothered	Control and Solution Suggestions
Anthracnose Irregular shaped brown and drying spots on the leaves	Mint	Water early in the day Thin out overcrowded plants If uncontrollable, remove infected plants and destroy
Bacterial wilt Dry, wilted leaves that appear as if they have been chewed around the edges	Sage	Remove infected leaves and stems
Botrytis Gray-colored mold on leaves, stems and flowers of plant	Rosemary	Ensure the herb is in well-drained soil with proper air ventilation
Crown rot Rotting spots by the crown of the plant	Angelica, parsley	Reduce watering
Damping-off Wilted, soggy-looking plants	Any number of seedlings	Increase air circulation and reduce humidity around plants

Disease	Herbs Bothered	Control and Solution Suggestions
Downey mildew Yellowish-tan blotchy spots on leaves of plant	Calendula, cilantro, tarragon	Remove infected leaves
Fusarium wilt Yellowing and curling of the leaves	Basil	Rotate plantings to avoid spreading Remove all plants at the first sign
Leaf spot Small whitish spots with dark centers covering leaf surface	Many herbs, especially lavender and nasturtiums	Remove all leaves immediately Keep plants properly spaced to avoid spreading
Powdery mildew Powdery splotches of white or gray	Bee balm, calendula, cilantro, lemon balm, tarragon, yarrow	Spray with baking soda and oil at first sign *(see recipe at end of chapter)* Thin herbs to increase air circulation
Root rot Plant will appear to be wilting; to check for root rot, pull up a portion of the root — roots with root rot will be soft and dark brown to black	Affects many herbs including lavender, oregano, rosemary, sage, tarragon, thyme and winter savory	Plant in well-drained soils and avoid over- watering
Rust Rusty colored spots on leaves	Bee balm, mints, yarrow	Reduce humidity and do not overwater Remove affected leaves immediately

Recipes for Homemade Insecticidal Soaps and Mildew Control

Pests and insects can wreak havoc on unsuspecting plants throughout your garden. Prevention can be the best option to deterring these determined little creatures. Unfortunately, many commercial and readily available insect and pest repellents contain harmful chemicals. When growing herbs for culinary and medicinal use, it is dangerous to consume herbs that have been treated with these potentially toxic chemicals. Using homemade insecticidal soap, however, allows the gardener to have better control over the care of his or her herbal plants. Also, insecticidal soaps are considered to be less toxic than commercially prepared insecticides.

Homemade insecticidal treatments are easily made by combining soaps with water and other plant-based materials to deter pests. There are myriad combinations that can be made from natural herbs to repel insects.

Making insecticides

To create homemade insecticides, start with an organically derived soap from your local health food store to minimize harmful chemicals. A simple recipe is to take 2 tablespoons of your organic dishwashing liquid and thoroughly mix it with 1 gallon of water. Put the mixture in a spray bottle and spray your plants where you see a pest infestation. To better bond the soap to your plant, you can also add several drops of vegetable oil to the mixture. By adding 1 cup of isopropyl alcohol to your mixture, you can create a very mild insecticide to treat scale insects like mealy bugs. The alcohol causes the scales' shell to deteriorate.

As an alternative, you can use a pure soap like castile soap instead of a dishwashing liquid. Herbs that have natural insect-repelling properties can also be added to your mixtures. By experimenting with different combinations, you will be able to find the blend that best treats your garden pests. Some herbs you can try in your mixtures include pepper, garlic, peppermint and vinegar. You can add these herbs to your blends either fresh or dried. You may want to keep notes in your binder as you discover which treatments work best on specific pests.

Additionally, some of these mixtures may also repel, but not harm, animal pests like deer. To deter deer from the garden, combine 3 tablespoons of hot sauce, 3 tablespoons of minced garlic and three to four raw eggs in a blender until well combined. Add the mixture to a gallon of water and use to spray on the plants.

By creating your own homemade insecticidal soaps to control unwanted pests, you can be assured that you are protecting your plants while limiting your family's exposure to harmful chemicals.

Mold control

Mold is harmful to the herbal garden as it kills buds, rots plant roots and wilts leaves. A fungus causes mold and grows in dark, damp conditions. A rainy growing season and extreme temperature changes can cause the start of mold growth as well.

Preventing and controlling mold in the garden can be done through the following steps:

- Remove any affected leaves, stems, or blossoms.
- Increase air circulation by removing plants that are overcrowded in the garden.
- If an entire plant is overrun with mold, remove it from the garden completely and throw it away to prevent the spread of mold to nearby plants.
- Be careful not to overwater plants and ensure that the garden has adequate drainage.
- Remove dead plant material, like fallen leaves, from garden beds.
- Replace mulch that has formed mold with fresh mulch.
- Trim plants and surrounding trees that inhibit sunlight.

To help control powdery mildew on the plants, you can try making your own baking soda spray. Dissolve 1 teaspoon of baking soda in 1 quart of warm water. Add 1 teaspoon of dishwashing liquid and mix well. To use, put it in a spray mister and mist on affected plants.

By taking care of your herbal garden through regular maintenance and pest and disease control, your healing garden will remain viable, become more productive, and create a larger harvest. The next chapter will offer insight on how and when to properly harvest herbs.

Chapter 7

HARVESTING THE BOUNTY OF THE SEASONS

arvest time is often viewed throughout the cultures of the world as a time to celebrate prosperity and reflect on the abundance of the season before winter approaches. Luckily, through growing your own healing and medicinal herb garden, you will be able to share in the continued bounty throughout the growing season. Often, the healing herb gardener finds himself or herself visiting the healing herb garden on a daily basis to take a snip here and there to use for the evening's meal or even to whip up a quick cure for an ailment affecting a family member.

Deciding when to harvest herbs on a large scale depends on the type of herb and which part of the plant is intended for use. Harvesting will also need to be done when the plants are at their peak flavor and fragrances. By picking young leaves throughout the season, the herbs will be at peak flavor and, ultimately, be more flavorful. On the whole, herbs that are grown for their leaves, like lemon balm, basil, or dill, need to be harvested before they flower. Once an herb flowers, it will lose some flavor and oftentimes, it becomes quite bitter. For the highest concentration of oils in an herb, the leaves will need to be picked when they are tender. This practice will ensure a high level of taste and fragrance. The ideal time to pick most herbs is early in the morning. Washing herbs prior to use may cause the loss of aromatic oils. Luckily, if you garden organically, there is no need to wash off herbs from the garden as the plants will not contain harmful pesticides. They may only need to be rinsed lightly to remove any soil or insects.

Flowering herbs, such as chamomile, lavender and borage, should be harvested just prior to their full bloom. Other herbs need to be harvested just as their seedpods begin to change color. Dill, coriander and fennel fall into this category. Ideally, the seeds should be allowed to ripen on the plant to reach their maximum flavor and fragrance. Root crops that are grown for their edible and usable roots, like ginseng and goldenseal, are best dug up at the end of summer into the early fall season. Pruning regularly throughout the growing season will also encourage new growth on herbs like chives, basil, mint, parsley and oregano.

An important component to harvesting medicinal herbs is knowing the proper techniques and tools to use on each plant, depending on which part of the plant you will be harvesting. Some tools that will come in handy for the harvesting process include:

- Hand snips, shears, or scissors
- Spade or shovel with a pointed end
- Garden fork
- Basket for gathering

Different herbs need to be harvested in different ways, depending on whether you want to harvest the roots, rhizomes, bulbs, whole plant, or just the leaves and stems.

Plant Part to be Harvested	Best Time to Harvest	Method
Annual roots	Throughout the growing season before it goes to seed	Digging up
Biennial roots	Fall of the first year's growth, or spring of the second year	Digging up
Perennial roots	Spring, fall, or winter	Digging up
Whole plant	During active growth or when flowering	Digging up
Aerial parts (leaves, flowers, seeds)	Depends on herb	Handpicking and snipping

Digging up Roots, Rhizomes and Bulbs

When looking to harvest the roots, rhizomes, or bulbs of an herbal plant like comfrey, garlic, or horseradish, you will need to practice a little patience. If you wait until the plant is at least two years old before harvesting, you will have a better yield to work with. The best time to harvest herbal roots is either in the spring or fall. Annual roots, on the other hand, can be harvested at any time throughout their growing cycle. Harvest the roots of annual herbs before they go to seed because the plant will often die once it is in that stage. Biennial roots are ideally harvested in the fall of the year they are planted, or in the following spring. Harvesting in the spring of the first year will produce too small of a yield for harvesting; by the fall of the second year, the plant will have already died. Perennial harvested roots like angelica can be harvested in the spring, fall, or winter. Ideally, herb roots from plants like chicory, goldenseal and ginseng should be harvested after the foliage drops off in the fall.

To harvest the roots of your healing herbs, you will need a shovel with a pointed tip or a three-pronged garden fork. If you are also harvesting the leaves and flowers of your herb plant, be sure to do that before digging up the roots, as you may damage those parts of the plant in the process. Digging up the root portion of your herbs is the most time-consuming part of harvesting your herbs for use. Exercise caution when digging up herbs for harvest so you do not cut off valuable pieces of the root or pierce the bulb. You will also want to harvest the roots of your plants on a day when the soil is evenly moist. If the soil is too wet, it will be compacted and hard to loosen the root. If the soil is too dry, it will be difficult to get the shovel or garden fork into the dirt to do the work.

To harvest the roots of herbal plants:

- Loosen the soil around the root area of the plant with a shovel or fork.

- Gently use the garden fork or shovel to pry the plant from the ground.

- Once the roots are out of the ground, trim off the tops — stems and leaves — of the plant to about an inch above the root crown. The root crown is the location where the plant grows out of the ground from the roots.

- Gently rub the roots free of soil, mulch and stones.

- Thoroughly wash and scrub the roots.

- Cut them into 1- to 2-inch long pieces for drying. *See the end of this chapter for drying instructions.*

- Keep roots cool in a refrigerator for up to 48 hours if you are unable to process them right away.

Harvesting Whole Plants

The method for harvesting the whole plant of a healing herb is done in much the same way as harvesting the roots. As with most things in your healing herb garden, before harvesting the entire plant, research the specific harvesting needs of that particular plant by referring to Chapter 3 on specific herbs or checking another credible book or online source. After gently loosening the soil around the base of the plant, use a pointed shovel or a three-tined garden fork to get underneath the root system of the plant. Gently lift the plant from the soil and shake off to get rid of any loose soil. Clean off the plant with the spray setting on the garden hose. The entire plant can be hung upside down out of direct sunlight to dry.

Herbs to Harvest Seasonally

The ideal time to harvest aromatic herbs, like lemon balm, is just prior to flowering. Many of the medicinally used herbs that are harvested for their flowers should be harvested when they are in bloom. Below is a guideline for harvesting herbs by the season when they are at their peak.

Late spring

Angelica leaves and stems
Borage leaves
Chervil leaves
Fennel leaves

Early summer

Basil leaves
Calendula flowers
Dill leaves
Lemon balm leaves
Nasturtium leaves
Parsley leaves

Sage leaves
Tarragon leaves
Thyme flowers and leaves

Midsummer

Angelica seeds
Chamomile flowers
Lavender flowers
Mint leaves
St. John's wort flowers
Yarrow flowers and leaves

Late summer

Bay leaves
Chervil leaves
Dill seeds
Elderberries
Fennel seeds
Garlic bulbs
Horseradish root

Early fall

Angelica root
Dandelion root

Harvesting Leaves, Stems and Flowers

Medicinal flowers and leaves can easily be harvested from your herbal plants on a regular basis throughout the growing season. When heading out to the garden to harvest, bring along either a bowl or basket to carry the harvested bounty. Flowers can be handpicked gently, or cut with very sharp scissors, being careful not to bruise the fragile petals. For stems and leaves, use the scissors. Do not pull leaves or stems by hand, as it can cause damage and may even uproot the entire plant. Gently shake any dirt or bugs off the flowers, leaves and stems. It is not necessary to wash these parts of the plant if you avoided pesticides throughout the growing season. By gently shaking them, you should be able to remove the garden debris. If you do not plan on drying these parts of the plant and will be using them fresh, they can be stored in a sealed plastic bag in the refrigerator until you are ready to use them.

Each medicinal herb is best harvested during different times of the growing season. Ideally, you will want to harvest the flowers of plants like chamomile just prior to their being fully opened in late spring to early summer. Preferably, the leaves, flowers, or stems will need to be harvested from healing herbs prior to the plant going to seed. If harvesting the seeds, wait until the plant goes to seed. Mint, for example, should be harvested for its leaves before it begins to flower. Harvesting at this point will ensure optimal oils and peak fragrance.

During the early summer months, you also need to harvest similarly growing herbs like sage and thyme to ensure additional growth throughout the remainder of the season. Another herb that flowers fairly early in the growing season is chive. When harvesting from the chive plants, be sure to encourage new growth throughout the summer season by cutting chives down about an inch or two from the ground. In mid to late summer, harvest herbs like basil before they set flowers to preserve maximum oils, tastes and scents. Biennial herbs like parsley, on the other hand, should be harvested during their first year of growth, as they do not flower until spring of the following year.

Collecting Seeds

For full flavor, wait to harvest seeds until they are fully ripe on the herbal plant. Caraway, sunflowers and dill, for example, will be at their peak in flavor and fragrance when the seed buds are about to burst off the plant. Ideally, try to harvest seeds just as they are about to fall off the plant. A plain brown paper bag is an ideal medium for harvesting seeds. Again, if grown organically, the seeds will not need to be washed prior to use.

To harvest the seeds from herbal plants:

- Hold a brown paper bag under the seed head of the plant.
- Cut the stem of the plant about an inch or two below the seed head.
- Shake the seed head into the bag to remove seeds.
- Gently pull seeds out of the seed head with your fingers.

Wildcrafting

Before the development of agriculture, humans would forage for food and medicines in the wild. The art of gathering edibles and healing plants in their natural habitat is referred to as wildcrafting. The term **wildcrafting** applies to gathering uncultivated plants wherever they are found. Wildcrafting is not necessarily limited to wilderness areas and can be done roadside, along a lake, or even in your own backyard.

If you are interested in trying the art of wildcrafting for medicinal herbs, you will need to do some research before getting started. This can be done either online or by finding an expert local to your area. *See Appendix C for some online resources.* Some healing herbs that you may be able to find by wildcrafting include dandelion, yarrow, nettle and wild cherry bark.

Some tips for wildcrafting for medicinal herbs include:

- Always ask permission if you will be foraging on private property.
- Bring a basket, garden gloves and a good pair of garden shears for harvesting.
- Go with an experienced wildcrafter the first few times to be able to properly identify medicinal herbs.

CASE STUDY

Blanche Cybele Derby
Wildcrafter, author, artist,
filmmaker and lecturer
wildweedcyb@gmail.com
www.tagyerit.com/freefood.htm
Books: *My Wild Friends* (out of
print); *More My Wild Friends*;
My Favorite Plants
Films: Edible Plants: Wild and Tame
(3 part series: Spring, Summer, Fall)

While picking wild strawberries in early June, Blanche Cybele Derby often comes in direct contact with poison ivy. The stem of the jewelweed plant is very juicy, and she breaks it open and rubs the liquid over her skin after picking to prevent a rash from occurring later on. Jewelweed usually grows near poison ivy, so it can be applied immediately. In case she cannot find any, she keeps a backup supply on hand.

To make a jewelweed infusion:

- Take several young plants and crush them

- Place them in a pan with water to cover

- Boil for a few minutes and strain out the plant material

- Allow the mixture to cool down, put into ice cube trays and freeze for future use

Not only is this plant helpful medicinally, it also has culinary uses. The flowers look like miniature cornucopias and add a touch of color to early summer salads. Another name for this plant is "touch-me-not" because its seedpods explode at the slightest touch. If you are able to grab them, eat the seeds inside — they taste exactly like walnuts.

"Plants have always fascinated me," Derby says. "In high school, I read whatever few books the library had that discussed practical uses for them. Unfortunately, there weren't many. Then along came Euell Gibbons and his Stalking series of books. That was just what I was looking for — someone who wrote as if he were talking to me personally and who had recipes on how to cook common weeds. I was hooked. I began foraging with a vengeance and have continued to do so ever since. From then on, I experimented with making my own recipes, often substituting wild plants for cultivated ones in conventional recipes."

According to Derby, wildcrafting means gathering plants from their natural environments for culinary, medicinal, or utilitarian use. She stresses how important it is to collect plants that are not rare or endangered and stresses wildcrafters should take what they need and no more. She also says wildcrafters should minimize the disruption to the plant's environment and leave enough of the plant to ensure its future growth.

"I really don't distinguish between which plants are medicinal and which are edible because I believe that my food is my medicine," she says. "Nor do I care whether a plant is wild or cultivated. If it is a part that's good to eat, then I'll use it. Many of my recipes use cultivated plants that people don't know are edible, like kousa dogwood *(Cornus kousa)* fruit."

Derby says foraging makes her aware of the seasons. She says many wild plants are only ready for a short time so she has to be observant to harvest them before their growing season ends.

"By using weeds as food, I'm eating locally and with the freshest ingredients possible; plus, they're not sprayed with pesticides. Doing this helps me lessen my dependence on corporate agribusiness — why should there be an industry between my food and me? I can forage for as long as I live. Any walk or bike ride becomes an adventure because I never know what new plant I'll find. Plus, it gives me an excuse to be outside and to be physically active. Wild foods are free and healthy. Everyone likes a bargain, and these edible gifts are excellent sources of vitamins and minerals. An added benefit is that they have some unique and delicious flavors."

To get started in wildcrafting, Derby recommends the following:

- The most obvious but important step is to learn which plants are edible/medicinal and which ones are not. Proper identification is the key that opens the door to plant knowledge.

- Start with a plant you already know like cattail *(Typha* spp.), which grows in swampy areas, and do research on it. Now that the Internet is so accessible, it can be an amazing resource for information, but be careful that the source is legitimate. There are also online forums where people swap stories about their experiences with plants.

- Guidebooks and films are a good starting point, but going out in the field with a knowledgeable person is by far the best way because you get to see actual plants in their habitat, smell them and maybe even taste them. Plus, you can ask questions and hopefully get answers. A good place to start is at a local nature center; often they have guided plant identification walks or they might know of someone who leads them. There are more and more herbalists in the United States who offer workshops if you want to learn about how plants are used medicinally. Several herb conferences are held in different areas of the country that feature talks/walks by experts from all over the world.

- Don't overwhelm yourself with trying to learn too many plants at a time; relax, go slowly. If you become familiar with just five new plants a year, then in five years you'll know 25 plants. That way, you can look forward to increasing your knowledge at a leisurely pace. After all, foraging should be fun!

Derby's favorite edible plants include:

- **Autumn olive *(Elaeagnus umbellata)*:** This very invasive but delicious berry is a source of the antioxidant lycopene.

- **Cattail *(Typha* spp.)*:** This plant has many edible parts. The slimy clear gel found between its lower leaves can be rubbed onto the skin to treat burns, cuts and bruises.

- **Chickweed *(Stellaria media)*:** This creeping plant, available in early spring and throughout the fall, is full of vitamins and minerals. Its leaves can be used as a poultice for conjunctivitis and minor skin irritations.

- **Dandelion *(Taraxacum officinale)*:** Just about every part of it is useful: leaves, flowers and roots. It is especially helpful for the liver and kidneys.

- **Elderberry *(Sambucus canadensis)*:** Syrup made from these berries is used to combat colds and influenza.

- **Japanese knotweed *(Polygonum cuspidatum)*:** The root of this highly invasive plant is a source of the compound resveratrol. It is also is being investigated as a possible treatment for Lyme disease.

- **Lamb's-quarter *(Chenopodium album)*:** This relative of quinoa is very high in calcium. The leaves have been used as a poultice for bites and to treat headaches as well as stomach distress.

- **Linden *(Tilia x europaea)*:** Tea made from its fragrant flowers acts as a relaxant.

- **Little hogweed *(Portulaca oleracea)*:** One of the richest sources of omega-3 fatty acids as well as vitamins A, C and E.

- **Stinging nettle *(Urtica dioica)*:** A nutritional powerhouse. I call it the "vitamin pill plant" because it has so many of them as well as high amounts of minerals, protein, and chlorophyll. It's been used to treat allergies, arthritis and countless other ailments. If you learn about only one new plant, this should be it.

Herb Harvesting Tips

- Provide new transplants enough time to adjust to their new home in the garden. They will also need sufficient time to develop and grow before attempting to harvest from them.

- Ideally, herbs should be harvested the same day you plan to use them for food or medicinal remedies. Properly store herbs that you do not plan on using immediately.

- Do not harvest more than one-third of a plant, and allow it ample time to re-grow before harvesting from it again.

- Sharp scissors are ideal tools for snipping off leaves and flowers of a plant as they will cause the least amount of damage to the mother plant and its leaves and flowers that are being harvested for use.

- For optimal oil content in leaves intended for drying, harvest herbs just before the plant produces blooms. Once an herbal plant blooms, its leaves will begin to wilt.

- To harvest the flowers of a healing herb, like lavender, it is best to cut the blooms just before the stem starts to wither.

- When harvesting leaves or blooms from annual herbs, harvest from the very tips of the plant by simply pinching back to lengthen the lifespan of the plant.

- Avoid harvesting during the heat of the day to minimize damage to the plants. Instead, try to harvest herbs immediately after the dew dries from the plants in the morning.

- If you would like to harvest herbal flowers for use in crafts, it is ideal to harvest them before they are completely open.

- Whereas annual herbs can be harvested until the first frost, you should stop harvesting perennial herbs about one month before the estimated first frost date.

- Herbs like chives, lavender and tarragon should be harvested for their flowers in early summer. To promote the growth of a second flowering, cut the plants down to about half their original height.

- Perennial herbs should be cut down all the way to the ground after the fall harvest in preparation for winter.

- If you plan to leave your tender perennials outdoors during the winter season, you should mulch them after the final harvest. Some tender perennials include basil, cilantro, lavender and parsley.

- Only harvest from healthy plants. If the herb plants themselves are suffering from disease or pests, you need to cure the problem before you can harvest healthy leaves, flowers, stems, or roots.

Below is a quick reference chart that lists when to harvest certain healing herbs. *For a complete list, refer to individual herb profiles in Chapter 3 or the Quick Reference in Appendix B.*

Herb	When to Harvest
Aloe	Anytime needed
Angelica	Leaves and stems: spring and summer prior to flowering Seeds: late summer Roots: early fall
Basil	Anytime needed
Bee balm	Stems and leaves: anytime needed Flowers: June or July
Borage	Throughout growing season
Catnip	Leaves: anytime, but best when plant blooms
Chamomile	Flowers: late spring and summer when almost open completely
Chives	Once leaves are about 6 inches tall
Cilantro/ Coriander	Leaves: when plants are 5 or 6 inches tall in spring or summer prior to blooming Seeds: summer through fall when completely dry
Dill	Leaves and seeds: mid-July through late August
Lavender	Flower spikes and stems: when flowers are nearly open
Mint	Leaves: anytime after plant reaches about 7 inches
Parsley	Leaves: anytime after plant reaches about 8 inches
Tarragon	Leaves: anytime prior to flowering
Valerian	Roots: harvest in the fall
Vervain	Leaves and stems: anytime
Wormwood	Branches: when plants are in bloom in the summer
Yarrow	Flowers: summer to fall when fully open

After the herbs have been harvested, any that will not be used immediately will need to be preserved properly for later use. Preserving medicinal herbs can be done through drying or freezing and suitably storing them.

Drying Herbs

Traditionally, drying has been an effective method of preserving herbs grown in the garden for later use. Dried medicinal herbs can be used in teas, tinctures, infusions and other herbal remedies. Because the properties of the herbs, like scent, taste and medicinal efficacy, can be lost through the drying process if done improperly, it is important to be careful and thorough during the dehydrating the process. The drying process should be carried out quickly. The requirements for proper drying include air, shade and warmth. When dried, herbs can be kept for up to three years, but should be used within a year to ensure full taste, smell and medicinal effectiveness. Because herbs can be destroyed by elements like air exposure, heat, too much light and bacteria, dried herbs should be kept in a dry place with limited sunlight exposure. Additionally, herbs with large leaves and high moisture content should be dried quickly to prevent mold growth. Some examples of herbs with high moisture contents include bay leaf, lemon balm, basil, mint, lovage and tarragon.

Herbs should be dried in a shaded and well-ventilated location. A large, empty closet, the attic, or an unused corner of a room, for example, would work. Other possible drying locations include a garden shed, barn, or covered porch. The easiest method for drying whole herbs is to simply tie the plant stems, with leaves and flowers attached, into bunches after harvesting. Keep one type of herb together in each bunch to allow for proper identification later on. Herbs will dry at different speeds, so by keeping herbs grouped by type, the drying process of each bundle will be kept more consistent. Each bundle should be tied together loosely by the bottom of the stems to allow for proper air circulation. Gardening twine, yarn, or even a rubber band can be used to secure the herb bundles. When tied together, the herb bunches need to be hung in a dry, shaded location. Rosemary, thyme, lavender, dill and lemon balm are examples of herbs that dry well through this method. Herb leaves are properly dried and ready for storage when they snap easily between the finger and thumb.

For a quicker drying method, the sprigs of freshly cut herbs could also be dried by spreading them over trays, a drying frame, or on sheets of paper on a table.

To Make a Drying Frame

Making a drying frame is an easy process and will cost much less than purchasing drying racks from a store.

Items Needed:

- Old wooden picture frame, 11" x 14" or 16" x 20", with the backing and glass removed. Another option is to nail four boards of scrap wood together to form a square or rectangle.
- Screen from an old window. You can also purchase window screen by the roll at a home improvement store.
- Four wood blocks to serve as "feet" for the drying rack.
- Stapler
- Wire snips
- Wood glue

Place the frame face down and lay the window screen over the back. Start at one end and staple to secure the screen to the frame. Pull the screen tight and continue securing the screen to the frame, placing the staples about an inch apart. Snip off any excess screen around the edges. Glue the four blocks, one on each corner, to the bottom of the frame and allow to dry. Turn the drying frame over and you are ready to start drying herbs.

Another option for drying herbs is to strip the leaves and flowers from the stems prior to drying. The leaves and flowers can then be dried on drying screens, trays, cookie sheets, or sheets of paper on a table. A tray filled with herbs can be set in a linen closet to dry with the added benefit of scenting the linens. The easiest way to dry herbs with seeds is to tie the herbs in small bundles and place inside a paper bag that has small ventilation holes punched in the sides. Hang the bags in a well-ventilated, shady area to dry. Conventional ovens can also be used as an herb drying method. Spread the herbs on cookie sheets and place in the oven. Turn the oven on to the lowest temperature setting possible. Herbs are dried when they break apart easily.

You can also dry herbs using a food dehydrator. The USDA offers instructions for making an electric dehydrator that you can use to quickly and easily dry your herbs. To make this dehydrator, you will need:

- One 4-foot by 8-foot sheet of A-C exterior plywood, ½-inch thick
- Nine 4-foot pieces of 1-inch by 1-inch nominal (¾-inch by ¾-inch actual) wood strips
- One 8-inch fan
- One set of five aluminum screen trays in the following sizes: 16¾x20; 16¾x19; 16¾x17¾; 16¾x16¾; and 16¾x15½ inches
- One pair of 2-inch metal butt hinges
- One ball chain or equivalent door latch
- Nine porcelain surface-mount sockets
- Nine 75-watt light bulbs
- 15 feet of #14 copper wire
- 6 feet of #14 wire extension cord, with male plug
- One 36-inch piece of heavy-duty aluminum foil wrap
- 116 1-inch No. 8 flathead wooden screws (you can substitute nails and glue)
- Eighteen ⅝-inch No. 7 roundhead wood or sheet-metal screws
- One 10-amp-capacity thermostat, 100-160 degrees approximate range
- One 4-inch electrical surface utility box with blank cover

- Two ½-inch utility box compression fittings

- Two wire nuts

The following is a diagram showing what the completed dehydrator would look like when assembled. *For complete directions on assembling the food dehydrator, visit* **http://naldc.nal.usda.gov/naldc/download.xhtml?id=CAT8 7213640&content=PDF.**

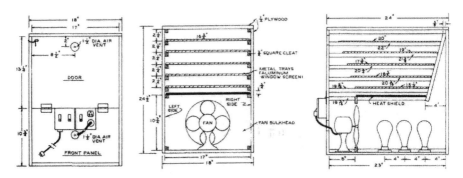

Image taken from "Drying Foods at Home," a USDA publication.

When the herbs are dried, they should be stored in a cool, dry location away from sunlight and moisture. Strip the leaves from the stems and package in airtight glass or heavy plastic containers with tight-fitting covers. Heavy-duty plastic bags can also be used for storing dried herbs. Be careful to avoid crushing the herbs in the drying and storage process to ensure the preservation of flavor and medicinal efficacy. The ideal temperature for storing herbs should not exceed 86 degrees, as the essential oils of the herbs will tend to evaporate at higher temperatures. Most herbs will keep for one to three years if stored well.

Freezing Herbs

Another popular storage method for freshly harvested herbs is to freeze them. Herbs that freeze well include basil, borage, chives, chervil, cilantro, dill, lemongrass, fennel, lovage, mint, oregano, parsley, sage, tarragon and thyme. To prepare herbs for freezing, simply wash and pat them dry. Spread the herbs in a single layer on a baking pan or cookie sheet that will fit in your freezer and place the pan in a freezer. Once frozen, the herbs can be moved to an airtight, freezer-safe container or plastic bag and kept in the freezer until ready to use. Thin herbs like chives and lemongrass can be chopped before freezing them. Aromatic ice cubes can also be made with herbs by placing freshly chopped herbs in ice cube trays, filling with water, and freezing. Herbs like peppermint and lemon balm when frozen in an ice cube tray make a nice addition to summer drinks.

Once the healing herbs have been chosen, grown, harvested and properly stored, it is time to start using them to create medicinal home remedies. The next chapter will detail the equipment that will be needed, the different types of remedies that can be created from herbs and some recipes for creating medicinal herbal remedies.

Chapter 8

USING HERBS

Preparing botanical medicines for home use from homegrown herbs is a satisfying and enjoyable pastime. Herbs grown in the home healing garden can be used in a variety of ways including infusions, decoctions, tinctures, syrups and elixirs, medicinal honey, compresses and poultices, infused oils, ointments, salves, balms, creams, soaks and as medicinal foods. The decision about which type of remedy to prepare will be based on a variety of factors including the specific plant, the shelf life of the finished product, the condition for which the remedy is to be used and the person who will be taking the preparation. For example, infusions and decoctions are good uses for a variety of herbs, but will require some additional preparation time for each use. Vinegars, syrups, elixirs and honeys are all effective ways to use herbs, but they also have a short shelf life, as do crystallized herbs. Tinctures are easy to use and have an unlimited shelf life. Topical preparations like salves and creams are convenient and effective with a longer shelf life.

Labeling Your Herbal Remedies

When preparing home remedies, it is important to accurately label each item. Labeling will make it easier to properly identify the product for later use and ensure correct usage. Ideally, each product should be labeled with the following information:

- Title, or name, of the remedy

- Ingredients used, including specific plant parts

- Recommended dosage

- How to use the remedy

- Cautionary warnings of dosage amount or people who should avoid the remedy

- Expiration date

Equipment and Utensils

Preparing medicinal herbal remedies at home will require using a variety of equipment and utensils, most of which are already available in the average kitchen. There is no need to purchase expensive equipment, but it is important to keep some key points in mind. Plastic, for example, should not be used at all when preparing or packaging medicinal remedies. Plastic has the tendency to break down and leach harmful chemicals. Only stainless steel, enamel, or glass containers and pans should be used. Copper and aluminum should be avoided as well because these metals can negatively alter the herbal remedy and its effectiveness.

Equipment to keep in your kitchen to prepare homemade medicinal remedies includes the following:

- Wooden or stainless-steel spoons (not plastic)

- Kitchen knives, in a variety of sizes

- Strainers, in a variety of sizes, or cheesecloth

- Kettle or teapot

- Saucepans, in varying sizes

- Glass canning jars

- Measuring cups and spoons

- Mortar and pestle or blender

- Bowls, in varying sizes

- Glass storage containers

- Good labeling system

With the above-listed utensils and tools from the kitchen, the following herbal remedies will be simple to create:

- Healing herbal tisanes: decoctions and infusions

- Elixirs, syrups and tinctures

- Medicinal foods (meals, crystallized herbs, vinegars, honeys)

- Compresses and poultices

- Topical treatments (infused oils, salves, creams, balms, ointments, butters, powders, repellents and soaks)

Healing Herbal Tisanes: Decoctions and Infusions

Healing herbal tisanes are a method of using herbs, as prepared in water as a drink, for their health and healing benefits. A **tisane** is simply an herbal tea prepared one cup at a time for immediate use. The general ratio to make an herbal tisane is 2 cups of boiling water to 1 to 2 tablespoons of a dried herb, or one handful of fresh herbs. Depending on the part of the plant used, the tisane will need to brew or simmer for ten to 20 minutes. Leaves and flowers, for example, will take less time than seeds, roots, or barks. Once brewed, tisanes can be enjoyed either hot or cold, depending on your need. Mint tisanes, for example, can be served iced during the hot summer months to revitalize and restore energy. On the contrary, a mint tisane served hot during the winter months can aid in clearing a stuffy head or sinus problems. Ideally, three to four cups of a tisane daily will help heal the ailment for which you are taking it. Tisanes can be taken throughout the day, in the morning to revitalize, or in the evening to soothe and relax. Raw honey or fresh lemon can also be added for some additional flavor.

CASE STUDY

Laura Mignosa, NCCH, AADP,
Nationally Certified Chinese Herbalist
Director, Connecticut Institute for
Herbal Studies
90 Wells Road
Wethersfield, CT 06109
www.ctherbschool.com

Founder and director of the Connecticut Institute for Herbal Studies, Laura Mignosa has spent many years studying and traveling throughout China, learning about medicinal herbs and their various uses. Her extensive studies and passion for Chinese herbal medicine led her to develop a program of study for other eager students in the mid-90s, during a time when finding a centralized place to study Chinese herbs in a clinical setting was nearly impossible. When Mignosa first opened the school, she offered classes on Western herbs, Chinese herbs and Ayurvedic medicine. Eventually, it evolved into its current specialization of Chinese herbal therapy.

According to Mignosa, the 5,000-year-old tradition of Chinese medicine tells us that we can stay healthy when we live within the confines of nature, or Tao, and live within the confines of day and night, Yin and Yang, and the four seasons. By preparing bodies in anticipation of the upcoming season, we will maintain balance in our health. Spring, for example, is a time to move in a positive direction after a long winter season. With that in mind, Mignosa offers the following herbal tea to help us move forward in preparation for spring:

- 2 parts He Shou Wu (polygonum multiflorum)
- 2 parts Gou Qi Zi (lycium berries)

> - 2 parts Bai Shao (white peony root)
> - 1 part Sheng Ma (cimicifuga)
>
> To make any Chinese herbal decoction like the one above, add herbs to 8 cups of water in a saucepan and bring to a boil, reduce heat and allow to simmer. Once the liquid has simmered down to 4 cups, strain tea into a large container. Add an additional 8 cups of water to the used herbs, boil the mixture, and simmer until the mixture boils down to 4 cups of liquid. Strain the herbs and add the two brews together. The first brew is to give Qi (life-giving force) and the second is thought to build blood. The tea will keep in the refrigerator for up to one week. Enjoy 1 cup daily.

Herbal tisanes are referred to as either a decoction or infusion, depending on the preparation method and parts of the plant used. Whereas a decoction is an herbal tisane that is prepared in water from the roots and rhizomes, barks, seeds, or berries of a plant, an infusion is prepared in water from the leaves, stems and flowers. Decoctions are gently simmered in the water, while infusions are covered with boiling water and allowed to steep, much like a traditional tea.

To prepare a decoction, crush bark or berries and wash, scrape, and chop roots. In a pan or teapot, bring water to a boil and add the herbs. Reduce the temperature and gently simmer for 15 to 20 minutes, strain and pour into a drinking cup. For infusions, measure the herbs into a cup or mug and add boiling water. Cover with a lid and allow to steep for ten to 15 minutes; strain out the herbs, or leave in the bottom of the cup to continue steeping.

Herbs brewed as tisanes can remedy a variety of ailments. Some herbs to try as tisanes might be rosemary to alleviate migraines and stimulate circulation, or lemon balm to calm nerves and aid in digestion. A sage tisane will help aid a sore throat, and thyme has been known as an effective cough suppressant. Another good throat and cough soothing tisane is violets and rose petals with a touch of honey. Chamomile, lavender and elderberries calm the nerves and aid in curing insomnia. Morning invigorating herbs to try as a tisane instead of a cup of coffee might include peppermint, rosemary, angelica, lemon verbena, or borage. An evening tisane to promote relaxation might include one or a combination of the following herbs: bee balm, basil, lavender, fennel, dill, or chamomile.

Elixirs, Syrups and Tinctures

Elixirs, syrups and tinctures are herbal medicines that are blended and taken orally as an internal liquid healing agent. Elixirs and syrups are created from a tincture base.

Tinctures

Tinctures are made by macerating, or soaking, herbs in either vinegar or alcohol. To prepare a traditional alcohol-based tincture, you will need the following items:

- A clean 1-pint glass jar with a tight-fitting lid (a canning jar, for example)
- 1 cup of chopped fresh or ¼ cup ground dried herbs
- 1 pint of brandy or vodka

Place the herbs in the glass jar and fill the jar with the brandy or vodka. Screw the lid on tightly and label the container with all of its contents and the date. Some herbs to try as tinctures might include echinacea and ginger to fight viruses, skullcap and catnip to reduce stress and anxiety, or dill and peppermint to soothe the digestive tract. Keep the jar with the herbs and alcohol out of direct light and store at room temperature for four to six weeks. Every couple of days, shake the jar vigorously and return to its storage location. After four to six weeks, strain the liquid by placing a clean cotton cloth or cheesecloth in a colander placed over a large bowl or pan. Slowly pour the liquid and herbs into the colander and allow it to drain for a few minutes. Fold the corners of the cloth over the herbs and press with the bottom of a cup or back of a spoon to push any remaining liquid out. The strained liquid is the finished tincture, which can be taken internally. Store the tincture in a tightly sealed, well-labeled clean glass bottle. The used herbs can be added to the compost pile. Tinctures made with alcohol will last indefinitely and do not require an expiration date. Tinctures should be stored out of direct sunlight at room temperature.

To make a tincture with vinegar, replace the alcohol with apple cider vinegar and allow the mixture to steep for two to six weeks. Finished vinegar tinctures can be kept for up to one year from the time the herbs are introduced into the vinegar. To ensure safe usage, make sure to include the expiration date on the tincture label. Some herbs that work well in a vinegar tincture are ginger combined with peppermint to reduce gassiness, thyme to promote good intestinal workings, and chamomile and catnip for positive energy for kids. Herbal vinegar tinctures make a nice addition to salads as a healing food.

CASE STUDY

Michele Medeiros
Herbalist/yoga instructor
rjmjmam@hotmail.com

Michele Medeiros is a yoga instructor and herbalist who has been practicing herbalism for about 20 years. She began her studies independently and apprenticed with Rosemary Gladstar, a renowned herbalist. Continuing to study independently and take workshops with other herbalists, Medeiros makes tinctures for personal use and also sells them.

According to Medeiros, a tincture is defined as an extract of plant constituents into a liquid medium such as alcohol, glycerin, or vinegar by means of maceration. She creates single and blended tinctures, mostly with alcohol, but some with vinegar or glycerin. Medeiros' tinctures are used for all manner of care and prevention of illness and well-being.

Medeiros stresses that you should get to know the plants you are working with. She also recommends that you never give a tincture that you

> have never tried yourself to someone else. Know how the plants taste, feel, smell and act on your body. Trust the plants and your intuition and always set a positive healing intention, she advises.

Elixirs and syrups

Due to their taste, elixirs and syrups are one of the easiest ways to administer herbal medication for health. Children and adults alike will be pleased with the taste and effectiveness of herbal medications administered as an elixir or syrup. Elixirs and syrups are made from a traditional tincture base.

For elixirs, combine ½ cup of honey, ½ cup of frozen or fresh fruit, and 1 ounce of a traditional alcohol-based (glycerin-based for children) tincture in a blender. Blend until smooth. You can substitute ¼ cup of fruit juice for the fruit. Any fruit should work, but avoid using acidic citrus fruits as they may create an unpleasant taste.

Herbal healing syrups were originally created in the 19th century to easily administer medicines. They can be made by warming 1 cup of honey in a pan over low heat. Add 1 to 2 ounces of a traditional tincture and simmer gently for about ten to 15 minutes. Remember to watch over syrups simmering on the stove as they can quickly boil over and catch fire. Allow the mixture to cool and pour it into a well-labeled glass bottle. Syrups will keep for up to six months and will need to be stored in the refrigerator. Administer syrups 1 teaspoonful at a time.

Some complementary blends for syrups and elixirs might include echinacea and ginger syrup to treat colds and flu, or St. John's wort, passionflower and peach elixir to support nervous system health.

Medicinal Foods

Incorporating medicinal plants into daily foods is not only a source of good nutrition, but also an effective method of therapeutic healing. Medicinal herbs can be incorporated as food through the use of honeys, crystallized herbs and vinegars, and can be included as ingredients in everyday meals. Crystallized herbs, for example, can be used as a candy-like treat or as an addition to salads. Medicinal honeys, on the other hand, can be used on their own to promote sleep and soothe throats, or as an ingredient in another food, such as crystallized herbs.

Medicinal honey is a syrup that is infused directly with the herb itself. To create a medicinal honey, heat 1 quart of wildflower honey in a pan over low heat. Add ½ cup of fresh or ¼ cup of dried herbs and heat for an additional 15 to 20 minutes. Pour the mixture into a glass canning jar, close tightly and label. There is no need to strain the herbs from the honey, as it will continue to infuse the syrup. Medicinal honeys can be stored and used for up to 18 months and used by the teaspoon or tablespoonful. Some healing medicinal honeys might include ginger for circulation, chamomile to relieve headaches, or lemon balm to calm an upset stomach.

Hildegard of Bingen

The abbess Hildegard of Bingen was one of the most influential and well-known healers of the Middle Ages. Known as Saint Hildegard, she was a German abbess, or head of a convent; Christian mystic; visionary; and writer of theological, botanical and medicinal texts. She believed that food and health were intertwined for well-being. Food, she felt, provided physical nourishment as well as spiritual energy to cleanse negativity from the mind and body. Hildegard's recipe for lavender wine, for example, was used as a remedy to detoxify and support the liver. Lavender, as we know today, is a cleansing herb that can also help relieve headaches, migraines, muscle aches, PMS, anxiety and insomnia. Because the liver is responsible for cleansing the toxins in the body, perhaps Hildegard's theory of lavender as a detoxifier may have been accurate.

To make Hildegard's lavender wine, empty a bottle of red wine into a steel pan. Add 5 tablespoons of fresh lavender flowers stripped from the stems and bring the liquid to a boil. Reduce the heat and simmer for an additional 30 to 45 minutes to evaporate the alcohol. Let cool, strain the lavender flowers and rebottle. Take 2 teaspoons of the mixture three times daily for up to ten days.

To make crystallized herbs, start by making a medicinal honey. Pour it into a glass baking dish and leave covered at room temperature for two to three days. Strain out the herbs and place in a single layer on waxed paper, covering loosely with an additional piece of waxed paper, and allow to sit for a week. The strained honey can be stored in a glass jar and used as a medicinal honey to add to cooking. After a week, sprinkle a light coating of sugar on the herbs and allow it to dry for an additional day or two. Crystallized herbs can be stored at room temperature in a glass jar for up to four weeks. They will keep in the refrigerator for several months. Try crystallized mint leaves to support the nervous system, angelica stalks to support the respiratory system, ginger to ease digestive issues, or rosemary flowers to promote circulation.

In addition to using medicinal foods through honeys and crystallized herbs, herbal therapies can be incorporated into everyday meals by including therapeutic amounts of herbs, instead of just to "taste" or season, in cooking and meal preparation habits. As well as being a delicious addition, healing herbs should be tailored to the specific needs of family members when incorporating them into meals. For example, people with stress-related health problems should include a healthy dose of oats in their daily eating habits because oats calm the nervous and digestive systems as well as inhibit the formation of cholesterol that causes high blood pressure. Others with heart-related problems will want to incorporate violet leaves into their salads. A medicinal salad, for example, is a valuable way to promote health while combining it with good nutrition. A salad that includes chicory and dandelion in addition to traditional salad vegetables, for example, will help support the liver and urinary tract. Add some crystallized violets for a tasty and heart-healthy addition.

Herbs can also be incorporated into a variety of meals including soups and stews, muffins, omelets and roasts. Dill, for example, is a great addition to soups, omelets and roasts and will aid in a variety of digestive complaints like excess gas and flatulence. Cinnamon and blueberries added to muffins will help support vision and circulation. Adding dill and fennel to breads will relieve heartburn and promote good digestion. Use infused oils on salads or in cooking to promote health in a variety of ways. Adding healing herbs like thyme or parsley to an omelet is a healthy way to start the day. *For more information on ways you can incorporate healing herbs into your diet, reference Appendix A.*

Soufflé-style herb omelet

Ingredients

3 large eggs
1/8 c. milk
1 tsp. of each of the following: parsley, basil, tarragon, rosemary, thyme, parsley
2 tsp. olive oil
1 tsp. butter
Salt and pepper, to taste
¼ c. shredded cheese, optional

Directions

1. Preheat oven to 350 degrees.

2. Heat olive oil and butter in a medium-sized oven-proof skillet (a cast iron pan works well from stove to oven) over low to medium heat.

3. Beat together eggs and milk in a bowl until well combined.

4. Pour the egg mixture into the pan and allow it to heat until the bottom is cooked and edges begin to form (about five minutes). Sprinkle the herbs over the top of the omelet and add cheese, if desired.

5. Place pan directly in oven and bake for ten to 12 minutes until nicely browned on top.

6. Remove from oven using an oven mitt or towel, being careful not to touch the handle or any part of the pan directly as it will be extremely hot.

7. Gently work a rubber spatula around the edges to loosen from the pan. Slide the omelet onto a plate and enjoy.

Compresses and Poultices

Herbal compresses and poultices are applied directly to an injury or wound and should be made fresh each time there is a need for one. Compresses can be used cool or warm depending on use. They are used to treat a variety of cuts, rashes, abrasions and even headaches. Poultices, on the other hand, are used warm to hot and are applied directly to help heal sprains, bruises and other wounds.

To make a healing herbal compress, first you will need to make either a decoction or infusion with the selected herb. Once the herbal decoction or infusion has been made, strain the liquid. The used herbs can be added to the compost pile. Take a clean cotton cloth and soak it in the strained liquid. Squeeze out the excess and apply the compress to the affected area. Reapply as needed. Use a burdock compress to help alleviate acne and eczema, dandelion for warts, and lavender for burns.

To make a poultice, take 1 cup of the chosen herb and place in a heat-resistant bowl or pan. Cover the herb with 2 cups of boiling water and allow the herb to steep in water until cool enough to handle. If the liquid is too hot, it could burn the user. Place a clean cotton cloth over the affected area and use a spoon, ladle, or measuring cup to apply the hot, wet herbs on top of the cloth. Allow the poultice to cool completely before removing. The used herbs can be added to the compost pile. Poultices should be applied one to three times daily and need to be made fresh each time. Always wash the cloth before reusing and never reuse the same herbs. Some soothing healing herbs for poultices include rosemary for muscle pain, comfrey for a variety of sports injuries, and St. John's wort for calming nerve endings.

Various Topical Treatments

An assortment of topical herbal remedies can be made from the healing herbs grown in the home garden. In addition to infused oils, salves, creams and balms, you can create ointments, butters, powders and soaks. Infused oils are a great way to get started in creating topical herbal remedies as they are also the base used to create salves, creams, balms and ointments.

Infused oils

To prepare an infused oil, you will need the following:

- A dry, clean glass quart jar

- 1/3 cup of dried herbal material

- Good-quality olive oil (enough to fill the jar and completely cover the herb). As an alternative to olive oil, you can use another plant-derived oil like sunflower, jojoba, grape seed, or sweet almond.

Place the herbal material in the jar and cover it with the oil. Leaving the jar uncovered, allow the infusion to sit for several hours to ensure that the herbal material used has not absorbed all of the oil. If oil has been absorbed, add additional oil to the jar. Use a clean piece of cloth, cheesecloth, or an unbleached coffee filter to cover the jar. Secure the material with a rubber band or canning jar lid ring, but do not cover with a lid. Occasionally, the herb will release gases that may pop the top off and create a huge mess. Allow the oil to infuse on a sunny windowsill for about ten days. Strain the oil into a clean glass bottle that you can use to store the oil at room temperature for up to a year. Remember to label the bottle with an expiration date and all the ingredients used. Some infused oils to try might include calendula flowers to soothe the skin, basil leaf oil to aid in digestion, and thyme oil for stress relief.

Salves, balms and ointments are essentially infused oils with a solidifying agent like cocoa butter or beeswax. An ointment has the loosest consistency of the three and is characterized by its pudding-like consistency, which makes it easy to apply. Salves, on the other hand, are firmer, contain additional amounts of the solidifying agent and seal the skin better to protect from drying out or allowing moisture to enter the area it is applied to. Balms are the firmest and contain the most solidifying agents and are usually used on the lips.

Ointments, salves and balms

To make an ointment, warm 1 cup of the oil that has been infused with the herbal remedy you want to use. In a separate saucepan, warm ½ ounce of either beeswax or cocoa butter until melted and add the wax into the warmed oil. To test if the consistency is right, place a drop or two of the mixture on a glass plate and place in the freezer to cool completely for a minute or two. Once cooled, the mixture should spread easily on the skin. If the mixture is too thick, more oil will need to be added. If it is too thin, more wax will need to be used. The finished ointment should be poured into a jar or tin. Cool completely before covering and labeling with all the ingredients and expiration date of one year from the date made. Salves and balms are prepared in the same method as ointments with the addition of beeswax or cocoa butter to create the desired consistency. Ointments, salves and balms are good for up to one year.

Creams

Creams are also prepared with infused oil as their base. To make creams, you will need to use a blender to create the right consistency. To prepare an herbal cream remedy, combine 1 cup of infused oil with ½ cup of melted cocoa butter in a chilled mixing bowl. Whip the mixture at high speed and add ½ cup of coconut oil. Continue to whip at a high speed until the desired consistency is reached. Throughout the process, the bowl may need to be refrigerated a few times to keep it chilled. The final product should be rich and creamy. Using a wooden spoon, transfer the cream into glass containers with tight-fitting lids. Label the containers with all ingredients, usage and expiration date. Creams will last for one to two months. If you live in a hot climate, you will need to refrigerate creams to avoid spoiling. Herbal creams to try include rosemary for sore muscles or calendula for first aid.

Herbal powders

Herbal powders can be used alone to treat skin conditions, taken internally, or added to medicinal butters. To make an herbal powder, a flour mill, blender, coffee grinder, or mortar and pestle can be used. Grind dried herbs using one of these kitchen tools to create a powder. Powdered herbs can be stored in a glass jar with a tight-fitting lid, out of direct sunlight, for up to a week. Remember to label each jar to ensure proper usage. Herbs that create useful powders include rosemary for its antiseptic properties, goldenseal to relieve minor burns, and plantain to alleviate insect bites.

Butters

Topically, medicinal butters made with powdered herbs can also be used to treat a slew of skin conditions including cuts, abrasions and rashes. Medicinal butters are prepared by heating 1 ounce of cocoa butter over low heat in a small saucepan with ¼ to ½ teaspoon of a powdered herb of your choice. Mix well and remove from heat to cool. Once the mixture has cooled, shape small pieces of the mixture into marble-sized balls and place in the freezer in a freezer bag or freezer-safe container. Label the bag with all ingredients, suggested usage and an expiration date of 18 months from the date that it was originally created. To use, remove one ball from the freezer and allow it to soften at room temperature in a covered container. Gently massage the butter on the affected area. Powdered echinacea root or marshmallow root can be used to create an herbal butter for infected minor cuts or rashes.

Soaks

Another way you can use herbs from a healing garden is as a bath or foot soak. Herbal baths and foot soaks can be used to treat a variety of ailments including hives, stress, respiratory and sinus infections, and to increase circulation. To create a healing herbal bath, add ½ cup of dried herbs to a washcloth and secure into a bundle using a rubber band. A muslin bag with tie strings or cheesecloth can also be used. Add the bundle of herbs to the tub and fill with warm water to your comfort level. Soak for a minimum of 20 minutes, discard herbs into the compost pile and wash the cloth or bag when done. For a medicinal foot soak, add ½ cup of dried herbs to a washbasin and add 2 quarts of boiling water. Allow the herbs to steep for ten minutes and add enough cold water to cool the soak so it is comfortably hot. Do not strain the herbs. Sit down and soak your feet until the water turns cold. Dry your feet and massage with an herbal infused oil or salve and put on a pair of comfortable cotton socks. Herbs to use for a bath or foot soak include: chamomile or lavender in a bath to calm and promote restful sleep; peppermint in a foot soak to increase circulation; and a combination of sage, echinacea and ginger to alleviate colds and flu.

Herbs for Pregnancy

The safeness of herbs used during pregnancy is an ongoing debate among scholars, scientists, healers and practitioners. Some argue that medicinal herbs should be avoided during pregnancy, while others recommend certain herbs taken in smaller doses can be effective ways of nourishing the body and easing it through the rapid physical and emotional changes that occur. It is recommended that you always consult with an expert, a naturalist, an herbalist and your doctor prior to using any medicinal or healing herbs while pregnant. It is the therapeutic and not culinary use of these herbs that some consider unsafe. In other words, a little cinnamon can still be added your oatmeal, but avoid using it in extremely large doses. Additionally, some herbalists do use some of these herbs for pregnancy-related ailments. Always consult with an expert before internally using herbs in a medicinal recipe while pregnant.

In addition to plenty of rest, safe forms of exercise and a healthy diet, herbs can help alleviate some of the more uncomfortable aspects of pregnancy. Nutrition, as a first defense, can go a long way in avoiding complications. For example, low blood sugar is connected to morning sickness and mood swings. Low levels of calcium, on the other hand, can result in high blood pressure, severe labor pains and backaches. Poor nutrition during pregnancy can cause anemia, constipation and contribute to preeclampsia. Therefore, it is important to follow a healthy pregnancy diet to ensure your body receives the nutrients, vitamins and minerals essential to well-being and good health.

In addition to consulting an herbalist or naturopath doctor, a good reference book can also provide information on using herbs safely during pregnancy. *Wise Woman Herbal for the Childbearing Year* by Susun S. Weed is one such example. In it, Weed suggests the use of motherwort to combat fatigue and mood swings. Additionally, Weed recommends ginger root tea to prevent heartburn and ease morning sickness.

Safe Pregnancy Herbs

Raspberry leaves as an herb are considered safe to use during pregnancy. In addition to toning the uterus and pelvic floor muscles, raspberry leaf contains high amounts of iron, calcium, and vitamins C and E. Raspberry leaf can be used throughout pregnancy as a tea to help prevent miscarriage, alleviate morning sickness, tone the muscles used during labor and aid in the production of breast milk.

Nettle leaves are another herb that can be used successfully during pregnancy. In addition to containing vitamins and minerals that help human growth, nettle can also help reduce hemorrhoids, ease leg cramps and decrease muscle spasms. Promoting a rich supply of breast milk, nettle can also be used after birth to help support the nervous system and stabilize hormones.

A tea made from fresh ginger root will help alleviate constant nausea.

Peppermint can be used at nighttime as a tea to help combat morning sickness before it even starts.

Children and Pets

In addition to offering healing for adults, medicinal herbs can also be beneficial to children and pets. Cuts, scraped knees, insect stings and runny noses are among the most common childhood ailments that can easily be alleviated through the use of healing herbs. Likewise, beloved family pets can suffer common ailments that can be soothed with herbal remedies that are carefully prepared and used.

Children

Herbal healing, in conjunction with traditional medicine, can be used to effectively heal and promote wellness in children. Always consult the child's doctor or holistic health care provider with any concerns or questions prior to administering an herbal remedy. Be sure to use extreme caution when using herbs in children. Always seek immediate medical help for any of the following conditions: a fever higher than 101 degrees, unconsciousness, severe pain, lethargy, stiff neck, recurring ear infections, difficulty breathing, dehydration, stings that cause severe allergic reactions, or severe burns.

An herb that is normally safe for use in adults is also safe for use in children. Any herb, like medications, can affect individuals in different ways. Similar to allergic reactions to strawberries or milk, children and adults can react adversely to a particular herbal plant. Always use caution and perform a small-dose test prior to using an herb at full strength. To test an herb and its effectiveness or adverse reaction, make an herbal tea and brush a small amount of the tea onto the skin of the child's (or adult's) inner arm. After 24 hours, if a rash, itchy eyes, throat swelling, or itchiness occurs, an adverse reaction is taking place because of the herb in question, so discontinue use immediately. If an adverse reaction does not occur, a very small amount of the herbal tea can be administered internally. Again, if adverse reactions occur, discontinue use immediately. If nothing happens, the herb is safe for use. Additional herbal safety with children requires that prepared remedies be kept well out of the reach of curious little hands. As with all medications, keeping herbal remedies in childproof containers and out of reach will ensure no accidental overdoses.

Herbal baths, syrups, glycerin-based tinctures (instead of alcohol) and teas can all be used effectively and safely for children. To determine proper dosing for children, consider the size of the child, the nature of his or her illness and the herb that will be used in the remedy. A child who weighs less than average will require a smaller dose, for example.

The below chart is a guideline, but be sure to consult an expert if there is a dosage question of any type.

Suggested dosages for children
When adult dosage is 1 cup, or 8 ounces

Age	Dosage
Younger than 2	½ to 1 teaspoon
2 to 4 years	2 teaspoons
4 to 7 years	1 tablespoon
7 to 11 years	2 tablespoons

When adult dosage is 1 teaspoon

Age	Dosage
Younger than 3 months	2 drops
3 to 6 months	3 drops
6 to 9 months	4 drops
9 to 12 months	5 drops
12 to 18 months	7 drops
18 to 24 months	8 drops
2 to 3 years	10 drops
3 to 4 years	12 drops
4 to 6 years	15 drops
6 to 9 years	24 drops
9 to 12 years	30 drops

Reference: Gladstar, *Herbal Recipes*.

Some childhood ailments that can be treated with home remedies include cradle cap, diaper rash, other rashes and colds. Cradle cap is a common childhood affliction that is characterized by a yellowish crust that develops on the child's scalp. An infused chamomile and lavender oil can be warmed and applied directly to the scalp and gently massaged in. Leave in overnight and gently massage the scalp the following morning to remove the cap. Wash with a gentle shampoo to remove the oil.

For a consistent diaper rash that is not deterred by switching laundry detergent, diaper brand, or reducing acidic foods, an herbal arrowroot powder can be used. As with all conditions, if the rash persists or appears painful, consult a doctor or holistic practitioner.

Pets

Due to increased pet care costs, herbal remedies for pets have increased in popularity in recent years. Like children, it is important to exercise caution when creating herbal remedies for pets. Unfortunately, if not careful, we can cause more harm than good to our pets by misdiagnosing, overdosing, or causing an allergic reaction with treatment. As in using healing herbs for humans, it is important to take great care when administering treatments to animals. It is recommended that an allergy test is performed on the animal prior to administering an herb to check for any sensitivity. Animals, like humans, have different allergies and are affected differently by various medications and herbs. To test, prepare an herbal tea with the specific herb you want to use and allow it to cool. Rub a small amount onto the back of your pet's neck and leave it alone for 24 hours. After 24 hours, check for any redness, swelling, or irritation to that spot. If nothing happened, the herb is safe to use on your pet, but always start with the smallest dose when administering. Always consult an expert with any concerns or questions prior to using an herbal remedy.

Healing herbs can treat a variety of animal ailments including cuts and burns, allergies, anxiousness and irritability, tender paws, and dry, flyaway fur. For minor cuts and burns, apply the gel from the inside of an aloe leaf to the affected area. If the cut or burn is serious, you will need to take your pet to a vet for immediate attention. For anxiousness and irritability, pets can be calmed through the same relaxing herbal treatments for humans. Some suggest to try include chamomile, catnip, or lemon balm infusions. Be cautious with dosing to ensure your pet is not overdosed. It is wise to start with the smallest dosage and increase from there to ensure no adverse effects. Internal herbal remedies can be given at the following dosages:

Weight	Dose
Over 40 pounds	1 tablespoon, 3 times daily
20 to 40 pounds	1 teaspoon, 3 times daily
Less than 20 pounds	½ teaspoon, 3 times daily

CASE STUDY

Samantha Davison
Rabbit owner and
rabbit rescue volunteer
rabbitsam12@yahoo.com
www.hopline.org (House Rabbit
Connection), www.3bunnies.org
(3 Bunnies Rabbit Rescue), http://
rirabbits.org (Sweet Binks Rabbit
Rescue)

Samantha Davison is an avid rabbit advocate and owner. In addition to working with a variety of rabbit rescue organizations, Davison is proud to share her home with a nine-year-old elder Florida White rescue rabbit named Nibbles. She works with a variety of rabbit breeds in her rescue efforts, from 3-pound Netherland Dwarfs to 20-pound Flemish Giants, and promotes the use of herbal remedies instead of traditional pet medications, as there seems to be fewer side effects with herbs than with conventional medications. Some herbal remedies that Davison recommends are rosemary and thyme to alleviate dust allergies and parsley for stasis (gas pains that are common and potentially life-threatening to rabbits).

When asked what made her switch to herbal medicines, Davison replied, "My vet suggested children's Benadryl to help with Nibbles' allergies — she would go into prolonged sneezing attacks. Nibbles really resisted taking it; she would struggle and get stressed out. I read up on herbs in a book called *Rabbit Health in the 21st Century*, by Kathy Smith, and decided to try rosemary and thyme based on their uses for nasal allergies and respiratory problems. She readily ate them. Within about a week or so of nightly sprigs of each, her sneezing had severely lessened."

Davison recommends the following for concerned rabbit owners:

- First bring your rabbit to a rabbit-savvy vet because there may be something more to the illness than meets the eye.

- Do your own research on trusted rabbit care websites or books.

- You know your rabbit best — if your vet's advice doesn't seem to produce any results, then ask his or her opinion on trying some herbs that you think might help. Most greens are all right for rabbits to eat, though you should do some research to make sure. There are also a few homeopathic vets around that may be able to help with dosages.

Occasionally, foreign objects will get caught or embedded in the soft pads of an animal's paws. Always remove the embedded objects gently and cleanse in a solution of warm water and salt at a ratio of 1 cup of water per 1 teaspoon of salt. Check the wound daily, as swelling or an oozing sore are signs of infection. Echinacea tea will help your pet's immune system fight off any infection. If the infection does not clear up quickly, or becomes severely infected, seek medical attention right away. If there is no oozing, the wound can be wrapped in a calendula compress to help it heal.

The following are herbal remedies you can use on your pets.

Echinacea tea

To make an echinacea tea, pour 1 cup of boiling water over 1 teaspoon of dried, or 1 tablespoon of fresh, echinacea roots or leaves. Steep the mixture, covered, for 15 minutes. Strain into a jar and allow it to cool. Use an eyedropper to administer to your pet the proper dosage by weight. Use three times daily for up to a week. If the infection does not improve or gets worse, contact your veterinarian.

Calendula compress

Calendula, when applied to wounds, helps reduce inflammation and promotes the growth of new tissue. Calendula compresses can be used safely on adults, children and pets. First, make a calendula tea by pouring 1 cup of boiling water over 1 teaspoon of calendula flowers. Allow it to cool so it is not hot, but still warm. Do not strain. Dip a clean cotton cloth into the tea and gently wrap around your pet's wound. Do not make it too tight as this may cause further pain to your animal. Try to keep the compress on your pet, if your pet will allow it. Repeat twice daily for up to a week. Remember to always use a clean, fresh towel and a new batch of tea each time.

Coat conditioner

To reduce the static charge caused by dry, flyaway fur, an oil conditioner made with sage will do the trick. Mix ¼ cup of olive oil with 2 teaspoons of dried sage and massage the mixture through the fur and skin of your animal. Rinse with warm water and dry gently with a towel. This is also a good remedy for a pet's owner who has dry, flyaway and static-charged hair.

As you practice with the different ways to use herbs from a healing herb garden, you will find that there are limitless possibilities to the healing remedies that can be created. An open mind combined with practice and trial and error will lead to a feeling of empowerment and control over one's health and longevity. The next chapter will overview the systems of the body and suggest some therapies to help promote wellness by using herbs you can grow in your garden. As with all medicinal remedies, always consult an expert if any questions or concerns should arise during the healing process.

Chapter 9

BODY SYSTEMS AND HERBS TO PROMOTE HEALTH

The human body is composed of several systems that work in conjunction with each other to promote proper function. When one or more of these systems performs improperly, it can throw off the entire balance of how the body works together. Included within the body are the circulatory, digestive, reproductive, immune, musculoskeletal, nervous, respiratory and integumentary, or skin, systems. Additionally, herbal remedies are beneficial to general first aid issues and dental care. Using herbal remedies can help promote health and keep the body in top working order. Herbal remedies should be incorporated as part of a healthy lifestyle and not relied upon as the single magic solution for wellness. A healthy lifestyle includes a well-balanced diet, exercise, stress management, good sleeping habits and a positive relationship with personal health care providers.

General Health

Maintaining a well-balanced diet, getting enough exercise, managing stress and practicing good sleeping habits are essential to achieving good health and vitality. By putting all these aspects together in practice, you can achieve a healthy body and mind and lead a productive, worry-free lifestyle.

As an effective component to well-being, following a balanced diet is a simple way to promote good health. Learning to eat properly and avoiding restrictive dietary plans will promote a healthy relationship with food. Implement the following ideas to improve your eating habits and your well-being:

- Eat as naturally as possible.

- Avoid overly processed foods like sweets, sodas and chips.

- Choose foods that are in season in your area.

- Eat fruits and vegetables of wide ranging colors. Each color provides different important nutrients and minerals for our body to function properly.

- Include nuts, oats and natural grains.

- Drink plenty of water.

- Eat several smaller portions throughout the day rather than three large meals to keep the body's systems running smoothly and efficiently.

Exercise is essential to good health. The human body requires the oxygen exchange that comes from vigorous exercise to properly revitalize itself. With most people working at desk-type jobs where they sit all day long, they become fatigued as a result of oxygen-deficient cells. By incorporating 30 to 60 minutes of regular exercise into daily routines, their bodies will become rejuvenated and have more energy to get things done.

Continued stress over time will break down body systems and result in the development of illnesses, aches and pains. Good stress management will help you remain healthy mentally and physically. Although it is impossible to remove all stressors from daily life, there are techniques that will help you manage your reactions to stress, enabling you to limit its damage to your body. Meditative practices like deep breathing, yoga and tai chi can have a positive influence on your ability to deal with stress.

In addition to a balanced diet, exercise and trying to reduce how stress affects your life, the body and mind need rest and relaxation to become fully recharged for proper functioning. Ideally, the body needs seven to eight hours of uninterrupted sleep. To help facilitate a restful night, avoid stimulating activities like exercise or watching television in bed close to bedtime.

In conjunction with living a healthy lifestyle that includes proper diet, exercise, stress reduction and sleep, herbs can also be used to promote general wellness. For everyday vitality and wellness, a combination of nutritive, tonic and longevity herbs can be used. **Nutritive herbs** provide essential nutrients and minerals for proper body function. **Tonic herbs**, on the other hand, strengthen and support various systems in the body. **Longevity herbs** help support quality of life so that people feel good as they age.

Examples of Nutritive, Tonic, and Longevity Herbs

Nutritive	Tonic	Longevity
• Flaxseed provides omega-3 fatty acids	• Dandelion supports blood and kidney function	• Milk thistle promotes antioxidants to slow down aging
• Bee pollen contains 22 amino acids, B vitamins, vitamin C and folic acid	• Nettle is good for bone health	• Gotu kola promotes mental function

Circulatory System

The circulatory system is a network of 60,000 miles of blood vessels powered by the heart that provide the body's cells with a required continuous supply of oxygen. In addition to oxygen, carbon dioxide and other waste products from the cells need to be carried along this super highway so they can be eliminated from the body. Common concerns that affect the circulatory system include hypertension, or high blood pressure, cholesterol/triglyceride buildup, poor circulation, stress and arterial plaque. For proper heart and circulatory health, it is recommended to incorporate the following into your lifestyle:

- Maintain a healthy weight
- Eat regular servings of fresh fruits and vegetables
- Drink plenty of water
- Incorporate foods high in fiber in your diet
- Limit salt intake
- Get plenty of regular exercise and reduce stress

As part of a healthy lifestyle, healing herbs that promote circulatory and heart health include oats, onions, garlic, flaxseed, astragalus and raspberries.

Digestive System

The digestive tract comprises a long tube consisting of a moist membrane lining that runs all the way through the body. Good digestive function is vital for health and well-being. The digestion process begins when you chew food and reduce it to a smooth paste with saliva to swallow. Food gets further broken down and absorbed as it moves through the intestines where the remains, or unused portions, are excreted by the body as a waste product.

Because your lifestyle can cause undue strain on the natural rhythms of your digestive system through stress and poor eating habits, your digestive system is constantly under attack. Very often people experience a variety of digestive issues like indigestion, diarrhea and constipation. Luckily, through adopting better eating habits, reducing stress and using appropriate herbal remedies, you can decrease the damage to the digestive system and promote wellness.

Different herbs can help support different areas of the digestive system. Comfrey, for example, can soothe and help protect the delicate digestive membranes. Raspberry leaf calms inflammation while lemon balm will ease pain and stomach spasms. Cinnamon and peppermint will help reduce gas. Angelica can increase digestive juices while dandelion and chamomile stimulate the flow of bile from the liver.

For indigestion complaints, an infusion of peppermint, dill, or fennel will help settle the uncomfortable pains caused by eating. If indigestion is a result of emotional distress, an infusion of lavender flowers will do wonders to calm the system. When confronted with diarrhea, keeping properly hydrated is important. Warm water with standard honey will help restore energy and prevent the body from dehydrating. Additionally, an infusion of ginger root and cinnamon powder will help reduce nausea and cramping. Herbs like fennel and raspberry leaf should be used as an infusion to help ease constipation problems. Like all health-related issues, always seek medical attention for severe or prolonged problems.

Female Reproductive System

Historically, women have relied on herbs to help balance their hormonal systems, balance PMS, ease the pains of childbirth and help regulate menstruation. Recently, science has caught up with the age-old wisdom of herbal medicine and confirmed that the ingredients in certain herbs, known as plant steroids, are similar to the body's own hormones. These plant steroids can help support and balance hormonal function by acting as the body's own hormones when there is a deficiency. In August 2010, the National Institutes of Health announced the creation of five botanical research centers, including one specifically for women's health, to advance understanding and further study how botanicals affect human health.

The female reproductive system includes the ovaries, fallopian tubes, uterus and breasts. Throughout a woman's lifetime, her body goes through a multitude of hormonal changes that affect emotions, mood and other functions of the body. Using a variety of herbs can help ease these changes and support the female reproductive system. As a caution, always consult with a professional for a serious condition, if you are pregnant, or if you have any concerns or questions. There are many herbs that are not suitable while pregnant, and it is wise to always err on the side of caution instead of risk complications to the mother and baby.

A variety of herbs and herbal methods, like teas and massaging balms for the abdomen, can be beneficial to women's health. Raspberry leaf can tone and strengthen the reproductive organs and their subsequent functions. Whereas yarrow and nettle can help regulate excess menstrual bleeding, cinnamon and ginger can ease menstrual cramps. To ease menstrual cramps, lavender and chamomile are quite effective, especially when used in a tea. Lemon balm and St. John's wort can help calm mood swings and emotions.

Premenstrual syndrome, more commonly known as PMS, is the name given to a variety of symptoms that occur during a woman's menstrual cycle. Lady's mantel and calendula, when infused together in a tea, will help regulate mood swings and alleviate headaches and bloating. If you find yourself tense and exhausted during your period, a lemon balm infusion will help energize. If symptoms are severe, always consult a professional for help.

Male Reproductive System

Allowing the male reproductive system to function regularly relies on regulating a life-long pattern of reducing stress to rebuild energy and promote vitality. The testes, scrotum, penis and prostate gland comprise the male reproductive system. Through the practice of a healthy lifestyle and the support of herbs that promote well-being, men can regain strength and energy.

Herbs can be used in a variety of ways to help the male reproductive functions. Borage or celery can be used to address exhaustion and low energy levels. Thyme and calendula can be employed to clear up any infections within the male reproductive system. Horsetail or yarrow will improve elimination to help combat any urinary issues. Ginger will help tone the sexual organs.

Immune System

The body's immune system protects from invading viruses, bacteria, parasites and fungi. Immune systems play a vital role in protecting bodies on a daily basis from the assault of outside invading microorganisms. The immune system is easily affected by energy levels and mood. Stress and tiredness will reduce the production of defensive cells, making people more susceptible to contracting an infection or illness. When the immune system is depleted in this way, the main thing that the body needs is rest. Herbal remedies, in addition to proper rest, can work to strengthen the immune system for well-being.

There are a variety of herbs grown in the home garden that can help provide much-needed support for the immune system. Echinacea, for example, will detoxify the blood and help renew tissues within the body. Garlic and thyme work to destroy harmful microorganisms. To help boost the body during times of illness, ginger and rosemary are the herbs of choice. To help reduce nervous anxiety that can break down the immune system, herbs like lavender and lemon balm can be used.

During times when the immune system has become compromised, herbs can be used in conjunction with rest to promote healing. Fevers are a natural part of the body's defenses to kill off invading microorganisms. Staying hydrated during a fever is vital, and an infusion of yarrow, peppermint and elderflower will keep the body hydrated and encourage toxin elimination through sweating. Echinacea can be used to help build back up the body's immunity. If a fever lasts longer than 48 hours, or consistently goes above 102 in children or 104 in adults, seek immediate medical attention.

An average flu will last seven to ten days and requires complete bed rest and lots of fluids. A tea made from fresh ginger will help support the immune system. An echinacea tincture taken three times a day will help boost immunity, and raw garlic cloves will have a powerful cleansing effect on the body. If illness persists or is severe, seek medical attention.

Musculoskeletal System

The musculoskeletal system is composed of the skeleton and the muscular tissue that attaches to it. A healthy and supportive musculoskeletal system affects how we move each day and depends on exercise, good posture and diet. The skeleton is the main support of the body and is made up of cartilage, bone and bone marrow, where red blood cells are formed. Additionally, the bones store vital life-supporting minerals like calcium, phosphorus and sodium. The skeleton also protects the body's vital organs: the brain, heart, lungs and spinal cord. In addition to regular exercise and a healthy diet, herbs can help support the musculoskeletal system in a variety of ways.

Herbs like rosemary, for example, promote circulation and help improve the blood supply to the muscles. To help eliminate toxins that build up in muscle tissue, cleansing herbs like nettle can be used. Comfrey can help reduce joint swelling, and yarrow can be an effective solution to easing rheumatoid pain. To reduce muscle tension, relaxing herbs like valerian or lavender can be used.

The majority of afflictions to the musculoskeletal system are caused by stress and tension, combined with a buildup of toxins to the system caused by poor diet. Poor sitting habits, bad posture, anxiety and emotional issues lead to muscle spasms and aches in the neck and back that radiate throughout the body. Muscle balms can be an effective way of alleviating pains associated with the musculoskeletal system. Some herb combinations to try as a healing balm include the soothing and pain relieving combination of chamomile and lavender or a combination of rosemary and ginger to stimulate the circulatory system. Lifestyle adjustments you can make to help support musculoskeletal health-related problems include reducing stress, addressing emotional issues, exercising and stretching in combination with a healthy diet. Always consult a professional for any severe or persevering conditions.

Nervous System

The nervous system is made up of the brain, spinal cord and nerves. It is a complicated network of communication linking the brain to the body to transmit a variety of messages. Stresses of everyday life can cause the nervous system to trigger its "fight or flight" danger responses and imbalance the nervous system, causing damage. When the body goes into "fight or flight" mode, blood flow increases to the muscles. If this continues to happen on a daily basis, it can cause the body to become fatigued. The most effective way to support and limit damage to the nervous system is by making lifestyle changes that promote rest, exercise and good eating habits. Herbs can also be incorporated as part of a healthy lifestyle.

Herbs can help restore nerves, promote relaxation and stimulate for more energy and better concentration. Oats and borage, for example, can help restore and nourish the entire nervous system. Chamomile and lemon balm will help relax and can help users get much-needed sleep. Herbs like peppermint and rosemary will help increase energy levels and improve poor concentration.

When the nervous system is in distress, it can cause headaches, low vitality and insomnia, all of which contribute to poor health and imbalances within the body. An infusion of equal parts peppermint and chamomile will help alleviate headache pain. For migraines, feverfew is a well-known herbal treatment. Passionflower, St. John's wort and borage can help restore the nervous system and restore vitality. A lavender and passionflower infusion can also help reduce tension before bed and keep insomnia at bay. If you experience severe symptoms, or they persist, consult a professional.

Respiratory System

Every cell contained within our bodies requires oxygen to feed on to create energy. Our respiratory system and breathing is vital to life. Breathing also helps balance emotions, aids in relaxation, and helps removes toxins through exhaling. Inhaling engages the muscles between the ribs, also known as the diaphragm, and assists in the air flow from the mouth and nose into the lungs. Exhaling, on the other hand, relaxes the diaphragm, deflates the lungs and releases carbon dioxide out of the body. Problems like colds, allergies and flu that occur within the respiratory tract are directly linked to the immune system.

Herbs that can help support the respiratory system can fight bacteria, reduce mucus and promote sweating to help eliminate toxins. Garlic, echinacea, eucalyptus and rosemary can all help the body fight bacteria and infection. Yarrow, sage, garlic and thyme can help reduce and expel excess mucus within the body. Herbs like peppermint can induce sweating to fight viruses and eliminate toxins.

The respiratory system can come under attack in either the upper respiratory tract or the lower respiratory tract. Whereas colds and sinus infections reside in the upper respiratory tract, coughing is relegated to the lower. For upper respiratory tract problems, yarrow and peppermint combined in an infusion will help alleviate cold symptoms. For sore throats, a hot infusion of dried cinnamon and fresh ginger with a touch of lemon and honey will do the job. To ease coughing, try an infusion of comfrey leaf with honey and lemon to soothe irritation. If the conditions are severe, or worsen over time, seek medical attention, as the problem may be serious.

Integumentary System

The largest organ of the human body, the skin, protects the inner systems and organs and enables us to touch and experience the world in which we live. Skin is an important organ in helping to detoxify the body thanks to the sweat glands. Sweat glands remove the toxins of the body through the perspiration process. Skin comprises three interacting layers that protect the body. Taking care of your skin is as simple as following a good diet, limiting sun exposure, drinking water, creating good sleeping habits, avoiding skin-damaging habits like smoking and exercising gentle skin care.

Herbs can help alleviate a variety of skin problems including blemishes and rashes as well as promote general, healthy skin care. Herbs like yarrow or chamomile can help reduce itching, redness and warmth caused by minor skin allergies. Thyme and echinacea will fight infections that cause rashes, sores, or acne, while oats can help promote healing of existing wounds, rashes, sores and acne. Fennel can be used to help balance the hormone fluctuation that causes skin blemishes.

Common skin complaints like acne, eczema and psoriasis can all be treated using herbal remedies. Gently and thoroughly cleaning with a dandelion infusion and then using witch hazel can help fight the infection that causes acne. Eczema, which is often complicated and aggravated by stress, can be helped with a cool chamomile infusion compress to calm the inflammation. Combining borage and lavender into an ointment will help ease chapped skin caused not only by eczema, but also by harsh weather. An infusion of lemon balm can help calm the internal system and reduce psoriasis.

Herbs for Dental Care

Instead of using harsh dental care products for teeth and gums, healing herbs can be used as cleaners, mouthwashes and for toothaches. Often, commercial toothpastes and other dental care products contain bleach and harsh abrasives that can do more harm than good. For effective dental care, try the following:

- Use a sage leaf to clean by rubbing it over the teeth and gums.
- Rub strawberries over the teeth to remove stains.
- Make a tea out of parsley, lavender, or mint as a refreshing mouthwash.
- For toothaches, crush cloves into a paste and apply to the affected area.
- Use chamomile tea to rinse the mouth and reduce gum inflammation.

- Use goldenseal tea as a mouthwash to help alleviate canker sores.

Problems in your mouth can often be related to illnesses in other parts of the body. With that in mind, it is important to consult with a dentist if symptoms persist or cause pain.

General First Aid

Herbs, when applied immediately, can provide quick and effective first aid remedies and are safe for adults and children. Severe burns, deep puncture wounds, broken bones, respiratory problems, shock, or copious amounts of bleeding will require immediate medical attention. An herbal first aid kit can easily be created from herbs grown in your home healing garden to treat minor injuries.

Things to keep in an herbal first aid kit might include:

- Aloe vera to soothe minor burns, sunburn, itching, and skin rashes

- Calendula flowers in an ointment or balm for minor cuts, sunburn, or eczema

- Chamomile in an infusion as a skin wash, cleanser, or compress for itching and inflamed skin

- Echinacea in a tincture for cleansing and boosting the immune system

- Yarrow in a salve for cuts, burns, bruises, bug bites, and stings

In addition to creating medicinal remedies for yourself and your family, you may also want to create products to sell and generate additional income. The next chapter will help explain the process of selling homegrown herbs and herbal remedies.

Chapter 10

SELLING HEALING HERBS

Growing healing herbs and creating herbal remedies for yourself, family members, pets and friends has the potential to turn into a business. With a resurgent interest in natural and local products, combined with an increased curiosity for natural, cost-effective medicines, the market is primed for such businesses. You will first need to decide if selling your herbs or herbal remedies is the right business for you. You could also consider simply selling your herbs and herbal remedies at local farmers markets to generate some additional income.

Best Herbs for Selling

The most popular herbs that sell well include:

- Basil
- Dill
- Oregano
- Mint
- Rosemary
- Lavender

- Bee balm
- Thyme
- Chives
- Tarragon
- Sage

Selling Your Herbs

Herbs can be sold in a variety of forms. They can be sold as potted plants, seeds in packets, harvested parts like leaves and flowers, as teas, or as healing remedies like tinctures, salves and balms. Other ways to use and sell homegrown healing herbs are in breads, dip mixes and soaps. Places to sell herbs and herbal remedies include farmers markets, craft festivals, yard sales, school fairs and roadside stands.

To get started with selling medicinal herbs, it will be necessary to do some research in your area. Start attending local farmers markets and fairs to find out what types of vendors are selling their products. Do you have something new and unique to offer? Take a notebook and find out who is in charge of organizing the vendors. Contact that person and gather the details on what you need to do to take part. Usually, there is a market master, or person in charge. This person will tell you about the rules and fees to take part in that particular market.

Once you find a market or fair to sell at, keep the following tips in mind:

- Arrive before the market opens with plenty of time to set up and organize the stand.

- Be friendly and willing to answer questions.

- Provide customers with a business card and a flier with information about your products and growing practices.

- Keep your stand organized and aesthetically pleasing to attract customers.

- Only display high-quality products. Clients will not want to buy a wilted plant.

- Charge fairly. Do not over- or under-price your competitors.

If you find that you have great success selling your products at local markets and fairs, you may want to consider turning your herb hobby into a business.

Is Starting an Herb Business for You?

Answering some basic questions is a great way to determine if starting a business is for you. The following questionnaire is designed to help in the decision-making process.

Questionnaire

1. In what form do you want to sell your herbs? As plants, or as freshly harvested leaves, stems and flowers? As medicinal remedies, or a combination of all of these options?

2. Why do you want to start an herb business?

3. How many hours a week will you be able to devote to starting your herb business?

4. Do you have experience running a retail-type business?

5. Who are you customers?

6. How will your customers find your business?

7. Are there any other herb-related businesses in your area?

8. Is your yard large enough to support growing herbs in bulk? Or, will you need to purchase a greenhouse, or rent farmable land?

9. Do you have enough room in your kitchen to mix and prepare herbal remedies?

10. Do you plan on hiring help or will you be doing all the work yourself?

11. What supplies would you need to start your business?

12. Where will you store the supplies and products you want to sell?

13. How much money would you need to get your business started?

14. Do you have enough money to get started? Or would you need to apply for a business loan?

If the answers to these questions have not scared you away yet, it is time to buckle down and do some research to start formulating a business plan.

Research and Formulate a Business Plan

In addition to determining if starting a business is viable for your lifestyle, it is a good idea to conduct research on your business idea and start forming a business plan. Find other businesses that are similar to what you would like to do. Contact them, let them know that you are considering starting a business, and ask if they have any valuable tips to offer. Most towns also have a local business owners' association or chamber of commerce where you can meet other business owners in an informal setting to learn about a variety of issues specific to local business owners. Good research will also come in handy when trying to formulate a business plan.

A good business plan should prove that your business idea is viable, that the business will generate a profit. The plan will provide you with a starting point for your future business. A good business plan will also be required if you need to apply for a business loan to get started.

A business plan should include the following:

- **Executive summary:** includes an overview of your business idea and highlights of your business plan. It is usually one to two pages long and effectively sells your idea.

- **Company summary:** includes a factual description of you and your company.

- **Products/services:** a description of the products and services your company will provide.

- **Market analysis:** summarizes your customer base, competitors, market size and potential market growth.

- **Strategy and implementation:** describes how you intend to sell your product and how you will put your plan into action.

- **Management summary:** offers a background on you and your management team, experiences and accomplishments.

- **Financial plan:** outlines potential sales, cash flow and estimated profits.

Unless you have previously owned and operated a business, or you have a business degree, putting together a business plan can be a daunting task. Luckily, there are a variety of resources available to get started. The Internet has a wealth of information on starting your own business, and it is relatively easy to find a business plan template. Additionally, there are numerous books available on the topic of starting a business. There are also a variety of software options that are specific to planning businesses. A good business-planning software package will ask questions and formulate a business plan based on your answers. Another more costly option is to hire a professional consultant.

Other Considerations

When weighing the options of selling herbs or medicinal creations, you may want to take into consideration the possibility of getting certified organic. Getting certified organic simply means that a USDA-approved third party, or certifying agency, will confirm that you are following the guidelines required to be organic. The third-party certifying agency will report its findings to the USDA for certification. Considerations include production methods, handling, storage and labeling requirements as demanded by the laws where your products are produced and sold. A valuable website for additional information is HowtoGoOrganic.com (**www.howtogoorganic .com**), which is affiliated with the Organic Trade Association. Additionally, the Organic Trade Association's website (**www.ota.com**) is another valuable resource for information on becoming certified organically. Both websites offer myriad information on organic issues and concerns. The local cooperative extension service in your area should also have certification information requirements available for your area. The Cooperative Extension

System is a nationwide educational network of regional offices that provide information on a variety of topics including plants and farming.

Another consideration when deciding to sell a medicinal product line is to determine what requirements your local health department has for your kitchen, or the space in which you are making your products. For example, some states require that the area used to create items for sale be located a specific distance from the main living area of your home. Any labels that are used must also meet U.S. Food and Drug Administration (FDA) regulations, no matter how small your business is. Because the regulations vary greatly by state, it is important to find out the specific requirements for your area. Contact the FDA for regulation information at **www.fda.gov**.

To get started with your own business, it will also be necessary to come up with a company name and get a tax ID for retail sales. Your state's website or local government office will be able to provide you with the necessary paperwork to apply for a tax ID and to register your company's name. If you are planning on having a website, you will also want to research available website names and register a domain. Additionally, you may want to consider becoming incorporated legally to assist with any liability and tax burdens.

Final Thoughts

Growing your own healing and medicinal herbs can be as simple as growing basil and thyme on your kitchen windowsill to as complex as starting your own business producing herbs en masse for sale. Either way, it can be a rewarding and fulfilling experience to grow, cultivate and create home remedies from healing herbs that you nurtured yourself.

For thousands of years, people have relied on the wisdom of age-old healing solutions made from items they could grow right in their own backyards. Luckily, we are seeing resurgences in returning to the earth for more natural-based remedies. Along with that, there is a return to the nurturing and farming-based cultures of the past and a willingness to provide for ourselves.

Planning, designing, choosing plants and caring for a healing and medicinal herb garden is a worthwhile endeavor. In addition to cultivating a healthy hobby, growing herbs and creating medicinal home remedies can generate some additional income. As demonstrated through the case studies in the book, there is a variety of ways in which healing herbs can touch our lives, from new career options to general well-being and caring for our families and pets.

When used as part of a healthy lifestyle that combines exercise, healthy eating and stress reduction, growing and using medicinal herbs can promote well-being and longevity as well as reduce the occurrence of disease and ailments.

ADDITIONAL HEALING RECIPES

Healing and medicinal herbs grown in the home garden can easily be incorporated into your daily routine through the use of medicinal foods, teas and bath soaks. Here is a sample of some of the recipes you might try with your own herbs.

Medicinal Foods

Medicinal salad

The ingredients for this salad support both the urinary tract and promote heart health. For added benefits, use a vinegar tincture as dressing. Serves 4 to 6.

Ingredients

1 lb. baby salad greens
1 c. dandelion leaves
1 c. violet leaves

1 tomato, diced

12 crystallized violet flowers

¼ c. raw sunflower seeds

Directions

Gently toss together all the ingredients and enjoy.

Heart-friendly pesto sauce

This pesto combines the health benefits of garlic, basil and sunflower seeds. It may be made and refrigerated for up to two weeks. The pesto can be added to pasta as a sauce or used at a topping for bruschetta.

Ingredients

4 c. chopped fresh basil leaves

1 c. sunflower seeds, raw and unhulled

½ c. olive oil

1 c. Parmesan, freshly grated

2 Tbsp. sweet butter, at room temperature

2 cloves garlic, crushed

Directions

1. Place all ingredients in a food processor or blender. Process to a puree, scraping down the sides often.

2. Transfer pesto to a covered storage bowl. Refrigerate for up to two weeks.

Antioxidant fruit muffins with healing cinnamon and honey

Ingredients

2½ c. whole wheat flour

3 tsp. baking powder

1 tsp. sea salt

1½ tsp. ground cinnamon

1/3 c. honey

1 egg

¼ c. milk

¼ c. butter, melted

½ c. blueberries, frozen or fresh

½ c. strawberries, frozen or fresh

Directions

1. Preheat the oven to 400 degrees.

2. Grease or line a muffin tin.

3. Sift together the flour, baking powder, sea salt and cinnamon.

4. In another bowl, beat together the egg, honey and milk. Stir in the melted butter.

5. Make a well in the center of the dry ingredients and pour the wet mixture in. Beat until moistened.

6. Fill each muffin tin two-thirds full. Bake 20 to 25 minutes until lightly browned.

Herb butter

Herb-infused butter can be used in any dish that would benefit from the addition of herbs: pasta, steamed vegetables, fish, etc. Herb butter keeps well in your freezer.

Ingredients

1 stick butter, softened

¼ c. dried or fresh herbs, finely chopped

1 tsp. lemon juice

Sea salt, to taste

A mixture of any of the following: tarragon, chives, parsley, dill, rosemary, thyme, sage

Directions

1. Using a fork, combine the herbs and butter until well-incorporated, adding the lemon juice and salt.

2. Place the butter on a sheet of plastic wrap and mold into a log, about 1-inch wide.

3. Wrap the butter log and refrigerate. The herb log will keep for up to a week or can be frozen for up to a month.

Fennel and dill oil salad dressing

Ingredients

18 fl. oz. sunflower seed oil (helps in digestion
and promotes skin and nail health)
4 sprigs fresh fennel leaves
4 sprigs fresh dill leaves

Directions

1. Combine the oil and herbs in a jar.

2. Seal and leave on a sunny windowsill for two weeks, shaking occasionally.

3. After two weeks, strain out the herbs and rebottle.

4. Use 2 teaspoons oil, 1 tablespoon lemon juice, salt and pepper to make a simple dressing for salads.

Teas

Cold and flu tea

Ingredients

1 tsp. peppermint
1 tsp. yarrow
1 tsp. boneset

1 tsp. elder flower

Honey, to taste

Directions

1. Combine the herbs in an empty glass or ceramic container.

2. Pour boiling water over the herbs, cover and steep for ten minutes.

3. After ten minutes, strain into a mug. Add honey to taste.

Tea to promote sleep

Ingredients

1 tsp. valerian

1 tsp. passionflower

1 tsp. skullcap

Directions

1. Add herbs to glass or ceramic container.

2. Pour boiling water over the herbs, cover and steep for ten minutes.

3. Strain into a mug and enjoy.

Immunity-boosting tea

Ingredients

2 tsp. echinacea root

1 tsp. hyssop

1 tsp. peppermint leaf

1 tsp. thyme

Directions

1. Place herbs in a tea strainer in a heat-proof cup and steep in boiling water for eight minutes.

2. Remove strainer and enjoy.

Emotion-stabilizing tea

Ingredients

To make this tea, you can use any one of the following herbs:

- Oat
- Comfrey
- Rosemary
- Mint
- Licorice (do not use if you have high blood pressure)

Directions

1. Add 2 tablespoons of any one of the above herbs to a heat-proof vessel.

2. Cover with boiling water and steep for 20 minutes.

3. Add honey to taste and enjoy.

Baths and Soaks

Herbal foot soak

Ingredients

1 Tbsp. wormwood
1 Tbsp. witch hazel
1 Tbsp. rosemary
1 Tbsp. Epsom salt

Directions

1. Steep all ingredients in boiling water in a heat-proof container large enough to place your feet in.

2. Once mixture has cooled enough to not burn the skin, place feet and soak until liquid mixture is cool.

Invigorating bath soak

Ingredients

1/3 c. rosemary leaves

1/3 c. sage leaves

Directions

1. Place the herbs in a small cheesecloth bag and add to running warm or hot water.

2. As an alternative, simply scatter the herbs directly in the tub.

Morning energizing bath

Ingredients

2 parts lemon oil

2 parts tangerine oil

1 part rosemary oil

Directions

1. Add this blend of essential oils to your morning bath and get a refreshing and energizing start to your day.

Other Uses

Herbal sleep pillow

An herbal sleep pillow is a small pillow filled with healing herbs that can promote sleep and relieve headaches.

What You Will Need

Fabric, 6 in. x 8 in.

¼ c. dried crushed herbs

Needle and thread

Directions

1. Fold the fabric in half with the wrong side out.

2. Sew around two edges, leaving one end open. Turn right side out.

3. Add ¼ cup of dried crushed herbs to the inside and stitch the opening closed.

4. Add the pillow to your pillowcase. As you sleep, the herbs will weave their effect on you. Lavender is a good herb for this project to prevent insomnia and aid in relaxation. A combination of chamomile and hops will promote restful sleep. For vivid dreams, try a rosemary sleep pillow.

Almond and oatmeal face scrub

What You Will Need

1½ c. oatmeal
3 drops almond oil
½ c. hot water
Ground apricot or cherry pit

Directions

1. Soak the oatmeal in hot water until soft.

2. Mix in almond oil and ground apricot or cherry pit.

3. Wet your face with warm water, apply the mixture to the face, and gently scrub.

4. Rinse with warm water.

QUICK REFERENCE LIST TO HEALING HERBS

Light Classifications

Shade	Partial Shade	Full Sun
Less than 3 hours of sunlight each day.	Three to six hours of direct sunlight each day.	At least six hours of direct sunlight each day.

Soil Classifications

Dry Soil	Moderately Moist Soil	Moist Soil
Needs limited amounts of watering and prefers soil dry to the touch between waterings.	Needs moderate amounts of watering and should remain damp to the touch.	Needs frequent watering and remains wet to the touch.

Herb	Zones	Light	Moisture	Soil	Start by	Spacing	Best Harvested
Aloe	9-10	Full sun	Dry	Sandy	Offshoot division	1-2 feet	As needed
Angelica	4-9	Partial shade	Moderately moist	Slightly Acidic	Seed	5 feet	Leaves and stems: spring and summer prior to flowering Seeds: late summer Roots: early fall
Astragalus	6-11	Sun to partial shade	Dry	Sandy	Seed-stratify and scar	15 inches	Roots should be harvested after the plants are at least 2 years old
Basil	Tender annual in most zones	Full sun	Moist	Fertile	Seed or plants	12-18 inches	Leaves: late spring and summer prior to flowering
Bee balm	3-9	Sun to partial shade	Dry	Alkaline	Plant division	8-12 inches	Leaves: early summer and early fall prior to flowering Flowers: cut when blooms are almost fully open
Black-eyed Susan	3-7	Full sun	Any	Low nitrogen	Stratified seeds	12 inches	Roots: spring or fall Leaves: throughout growing season
Boneset	4-8	Full sun	Moist	Sandy or clay-like	Seed or cuttings	24-30 inches	When in full bloom
Borage	Hardy annual, all zones	Full sun	Moist	Any	Seed	2 feet	Throughout growing season
Calendula	Hardy annual, all	Full sun	Moderately moist	Any	Seed or plant	10 inches	Flowers: throughout spring and summer
California poppy	All zones; best in 6-11	Sunny	Dry	Poor	Seed	10-12 inches	Flowers and seed pods: when in full bloom

Herb	Zones	Light	Moisture	Soil	Start by	Spacing	Best Harvested
Catnip	3-9	Full sun	Moderately moist	Any	Stratified seed or root	8 inches	Leaves: anytime, but best when plant blooms
Cayenne	7-11	Full sun	Dry	Any	Seed	12 inches	Late summer to early fall when chilies turn red
Celery	5 and higher	Full sun	Moist	Fertile	Stratified and soaked overnight seeds	12 inches	When stalks reach 1 foot in height
Chamomile	4-9	Partial shade	Dry	Sandy	Seed or root division	6 inches	When flowers are in bloom
Chicory	3-10	Full sun	Dry	Any	Stratified seed	10 inches	Roots: spring and fall Flowers and leaves: throughout growing season
Chives	3-10	Full to partial sun	Any	Any	Seed or crown division	6-9 inches	Once stalks are about 6 inches tall and turn green
Chrysanthemum	3-9	Full sun	Dry	Fertile	Seed, cuttings or root division	18 inches	Flowers: when in full bloom
Cilantro / Coriander	3 and higher	Full sun	Dry	Any	Seed	8-10 inches	Leaves: when plants are 5 or 6 inches tall in spring or summer prior to blooming Seeds: summer through fall when completely dry
Cinnamon	9-11	Full sun	Moist	Fertile	Root	30-40 feet	Bark: after 2 years of growth
Comfrey	3-9	Full sun	Moist	Any	Root division	3 feet	Leaves: spring and summer Roots: fall
Corn	Any	Full sun	Moist	Fertile	Seed	2 to 3 feet	Fall, when the silks begin to turn brown
Dandelion	Any	Anywhere	Anywhere	Any	Seed	10-12 inches	Any time

Herb	Zones	Light	Moisture	Soil	Start by	Spacing	Best Harvested
Dill	Any	Full sun	Average	Moderately fertile	Seed	12-15 inches	Leaves: when plants are young Seeds: before seed head turns brown
Echinacea	3-9	Full sun	Moist	Any	Seed	12 inches	Flowers: anytime throughout growing season Roots: in the fall 2-3 years after planting
Elder	4-9	Partial sun	Moist	Fertile	Hardwood cuttings	6-10 inches	Fruit: July through August Flowers: anytime during season
Elecampane	4-9	Partial shade	Moderately moist	Loamy	Stratified seeds	36 inches	Roots: spring or fall
Fennel	4-10	Full sun	Moderately dry	Moderately fertile	Seed	12 inches	Roots: spring or fall Leaves: anytime Seeds: when ripe
Feverfew	4-9	Full sun	Moderately moist	Any	Seed	12 inches	Leaves just prior to blooming
Flaxseed	3-9	Full sun	Moderately moist	Fertile	Seed	10-12	Seeds: when about a third have turned brown
Garlic	All	Full sun	Moderately moist	Fertile	Bulb	6 inches	When lower leaves turn brown
Ginger	9-11	Shade or partial shade	Moist	Fertile	Root propagation	12 inches	4-9 months after planting
Goldenseal	5-8	Partial shade	Moderately moist	Any	Root divisions	10 inches	Roots: in the fall 4-5 years after planting
Gotu kola	8-11	Partial shade	Moderately moist	Loamy	Root divisions	12-14 inches	During hot seasons

Herb	Zones	Light	Moisture	Soil	Start by	Spacing	Best Harvested
Hibiscus	9-10 out-doors 1-8 in-doors	Full sun	Moder-ately dry	Sandy	Layering cutting	3-6 feet	Flowers: in full bloom
Hops	4-8	Partial shade	Moder-ately dry	Average	Root cuttings	3 feet	Flower clusters: late summer to early fall
Horseradish	4-9	Full sun	Mod-erately moist	Mod-erately fertile	Root division	2 feet	Root: Spring following year after planting
Hyssop	4-9	Full sun	Dry	Sandy	Seed	6-12 inches	Just prior to blooming
Lavender	5-8	Full sun	Dry	Fertile sandy	Seed or plant	3 feet	Flower spikes and stems: when flowers are nearly open
Lemon balm	4-9	Full sun	Moder-ately dry	Mod-erately fertile	Seed Root division	12-15 inches	Leaves: anytime during growing season
Lemon verbena	9-10	Sun partial shade	Mod-erately moist	Fertile	Cuttings	12-15 inches	Leaves and stems: once stems reach 8 inches tall Flowers: anytime throughout growing season
Lemongrass	8-11	Full sun	Moder-ately dry	Sandy	Seed	36-40 inches	Leaves and shoots: mid to late summer
Licorice	9-11	Full sun to partial shade	Mod-erately moist	Any	Stratified seeds	2 feet	Spring or fall of its 3rd year of growth
Lovage	5-8	Partial shade	Moist	Mod-erately fertile	Stratified seeds	24 inches	Leaves: prior to flowering Seed heads: late summer Roots: spring or fall
Marshmallow	5-8	Sun to partial shade	Mod-erately moist	Loamy	Seeds cuttings	12 inches	Roots: spring or fall Leaves and flowers: anytime
Milk thistle	6-9	Full sun	Dry	Any	Seed	12-15 inches	Seeds: when they turn brown

Herb	Zones	Light	Moisture	Soil	Start by	Spacing	Best Harvested
Mints	5-9	Partial shade	Moist	Any	Stem cutting Root cutting	18 inches	Leaves: anytime when plant reaches about 7 inches
Motherwort	4-8	Full sun to partial shade	Moderately moist	Any	Stratified seeds	15-20 inches	Leaves and stems: anytime throughout growing season
Mullein	3-9	Full sun	Moderately moist	Any	Seed	15 inches	Leaves and flowers: anytime Roots: fall of 1st year or spring of 2nd
Nasturtium	Any	Full sun	Moderately moist	Moderately fertile	Seed	12 inches	Leaves and stems: when plant is 6 inches tall Flowers: throughout season Seeds: when ¼ inch in diameter
Nettle	5-9	Any	Moist	Fertile	Seed	12 inches	Prior to flowering
Oat	Any	Full sun	Dry	Any	Seed	1 inch	Seeds and stalks: when plant is green
Onion	Any	Full sun	Moist	Loamy	Bulb	3-4 inches	When half of the stalks have tipped over
Oregano	5-9	Full sun	Dry	Any	Seeds Stem cuttings	12 inches	Anytime throughout growing season
Parsley	6-11	Full sun	Moist	Fertile	Seed	6-8 inches	Leaves: anytime after plant has grown to about 8 inches
Passionflower	5-9	Shade to partial shade	Moist	Fertile	Seed cuttings Root division	18 inches	Flowers, leaves, fruit: anytime during growing season
Plantain	3-8	Full sun	Moderately moist	Any	Seed	12 inches	Whole plant at any time
Pumpkin	Any	Full sun	Moderately moist	Moderately fertile	Seed	6-8 inches	Fruit: fall

Herb	Zones	Light	Moisture	Soil	Start by	Spacing	Best Harvested
Red clover	5-9	Full sun to partial shade	Moderately moist	Any	Seed	12 inches	Flowers: throughout season
Red raspberry	3-8	Full sun to partial shade	Moist	Fertile	Canes	3 feet	Leaves: throughout season Fruit: when red and ripe
Rosemary	8-11	Full sun	Dry	Fertile Sandy	Cuttings	18 inches	Stems and leaves: anytime
Sage	5-9	Full sun to partial shade	Moderately moist	Moderately fertile	Seed	36 inches	After 1st year of growth, harvest leaves anytime throughout season
Self-heal	4-9	Full sun to partial shade	Moderately dry	Humus	Stratified seeds	6-9 inches	Flowers: when in bloom
Sheep sorrel	3-9	Full sun	Moderately moist	Any	Seed	12 inches	Flowers, leaves, stems: anytime throughout growing season
Shepherd's purse	Any	Full sun	Moderately moist	Any	Seed	10 inches	Flowers, leaves, and stems: when in full bloom
Skullcap	4-8	Full sun or partial shade	Moderately moist	Any	Seed	12 inches	Flowers, leaves, and stems: anytime throughout growing season
St John's wort	3-9	Any	Moderately moist	Any	Seed Root division	18-36 inches	Flowers: when in bloom
Stevia	9-11 as perennial, any as annual	Full sun or partial shade	Moderately dry	Fertile	Cuttings or purchase plant	18-24 inches	Flowers, leaves, stems: throughout growing season
Strawberry	3-8	Full sun or partial shade	Moist	Fertile	Plants	12-18 inches	Leaves: throughout season Berries: throughout growing season when red and ripe

Herb	Zones	Light	Moisture	Soil	Start by	Spacing	Best Harvested
Sunflowers	Any	Full sun	Moderately moist	Moderately fertile	Seed	Depends on variety	Roots: fall when growing season is over Seed heads: once the flower begins to die back
Tarragon	4-8	Full sun or partial shade	Moderately moist	Moderately fertile	Root propagation	18-24 inches	Leaves: anytime
Thyme	5-9	Full sun to partial shade	Moderately dry	Moderately fertile	Seed Root cuttings	10-12 inches	Leaves: anytime
Valerian	3-9	Partial shade	Moist	Fertile	Seed Runner Crown division	36 inches	Roots: harvest in the fall
Vervain	5-9	Full sun	Moderately dry	Moderately fertile	Seed Stem cuttings	12 inches	Leaves and stems: anytime
Violet	3-7	Shade	Moderately moist	Fertile	Plant	12 inches	Flowers: when in full bloom Leaves: throughout growing season Roots: fall
Witch hazel	3-9	Full sun	Moist	Acidic	Plant	20 feet	Fall and winter
Wormwood	4-6	Full sun to partial shade	Moderately moist	Moderately fertile	Seed Semi-hard cuttings	15 inches	Branches: when plants are in bloom in the summer
Yarrow	2-8	Full sun	Moderately moist	Fertile	Root division seed	18 inches	Flowers: summer to fall when fully open
Yerba mansa	8-9	Full sun	Moist	Salty	Seed Root cuttings	12 inches	Flowers: during growing season Roots: fall

Appendix C

RESOURCES

Healing Herb Resources

20,000 Secrets of Tea: The Most Effective Ways to Benefit from Nature's Healing Herbs by Victoria Zak

Family Herbal: A Guide to Living Life with Energy, Health, and Vitality by Rosemary Gladstar

Herbs for Pets: The Natural Way to Enhance Your Pet's Life by Mary L. Wulff

The Old Farmer's Almanac

Wise Woman Herbal for the Childbearing Year by Susun S. Weed

Professional Herbal Associations

For information on growing and using herbs, consult the following websites for additional information:

American Herb Association
www.ahaherb.com

American Herbalists Guild
ahgoffice@earthlink.net
http://americanherbalistsguild.com

Academy of Integrative Health and Medicine
https://aihm.org/ahma-welcome-aihm

The Herb Growing and Marketing Network
www.herbworld.com

Seed, Plant, and Gardening Supplies

The following are resources for seeds, plants, books and tools for herbs:

Bountiful Gardens
www.bountifulgardens.org
Bountiful Gardens sells organically grown herb and vegetable seeds.

The Cook's Garden
www.cooksgarden.com
The Cook's Garden sells culinary vegetable and herb seeds, books
and supplies.

Horizon Herbs
www.horizonherbs.com
Horizon Herbs sells seeds and bare roots.

Le Jardin du Gourmet
www.artisticgardens.com
Le Jardin du Gourmet sells herb seeds and books.

Peaceful Valley Farm and Garden Supply
www.groworganic.com
Peaceful Valley Farm and Garden Supply sells pest and insect controls,
fertilizers, tools, seeds, irrigation and greenhouse supplies.

E.D. Luce Packaging
www.essentialsupplies.com
E.D. Luce Packaging offers wholesale bottles, vials, jars and apothecary supplies by the case.

Mountain Rose Herbs
www.mountainroseherbs.com
Mountain Rose Herbs sells a variety of medicine-making supplies, bottles, beeswax, oils and more.

Educational Resources

For additional information on herbs, growing herbs, organic certification, lunar gardening, or small businesses, contact one of the following organizations:

Cooperative Extension System
http://nifa.usda.gov/extension

Herb Research Foundation
www.herbs.org

U.S. Food and Drug Administration (FDA)
www.fda.gov

U.S. Small Business Administration
www.sba.gov

Organic Trade Association
www.ota.com

Gardening by the Moon
www.gardeningbythemoon.com

Glossary

Annuals: plants that are started from seed, grow, and die within a one-year cycle

Antioxidants: substances that many believe delay cell damage caused by free radicals

Biennials: plants that require two years to complete their growth cycle

Blanching: the act of plunging an herb in boiling water for several minutes

Chaff: remaining pieces of a seed covering that stay attached to the seed

Container gardening: growing a plant in a container instead of sowing it directly into the ground

Crown: the top part of a plant that sticks out of the soil

Decoction: a stronger and more concentrated version of an infusion

Evergreen: a plant with foliage that remains green throughout the year

Flavonoids: plant compounds with antioxidant properties that benefit cell health

Free radicals: damaging by-products that are created when cells use oxygen

Full sun: a garden location that receives at least six hours of direct sunlight each day

Growing zone: a geographically determined region that defines which category of plants will be able to grow in a specific region

Hardiness: the average minimum temperatures a perennial plant can survive in

Hardwood cutting: taking cuttings from the fully mature wood of a plant's stem base in mid- to late autumn

Herbaceous plants: non-woody plants that have soft, green stems

Herbalist: someone who is specially trained in herbal medicine and uses plants and natural substances to prevent and treat illness and improve health and healing

Infusion: a healing remedy created when herbs are soaked or boiled in water

Loamy soil: a soil combination that has sand, silt, clay, and organic matter

Longevity herbs: herbs that support quality of life so people feel good as they age

Naturopathic doctor: a primary care doctor trained in treating the whole person through the use natural methods to prevent and treat disease

Nutritive herbs: herbs that provide essential nutrients and minerals for proper bodily functions

Partial shade: a garden location that receives only three to six hours of direct sunlight each day

Perennial: a plant that has an above-ground portion that dies in the winter and grows back each spring

Rhizomatous plants: herbs with a branching root system that grows laterally underground

Root division: the process of separating plants at the root base to create more than one plant

Rooting hormone: a substance used to stimulate root growth

Semi-ripe cutting: taking cuttings from a plant in midsummer

Shade: a garden location that receives less than three hours of sunlight each day

Softwood cutting: taking cuttings from the new growth on a plant in mid-spring to early summer

Strobiles: flower clusters

Tannins: plant compounds that exert high antioxidant activity and offer protection to the gastrointestinal tract

Taproot: a large root structure that goes deep into the ground and has many smaller roots growing off the main root base

Tiller: a garden tool with wheels and sharp spikes used to plow or mix soil

Tincture: a healing solution made by steeping herbs in alcohol or vinegar

Tisane: an herbal tea prepared one cup at a time for immediate use

Tonic herbs: herbs that strengthen and support various systems in the body

Vegetative propagation: a method of creating new plants from cuttings of existing plants

Wildcrafting: the process of gathering uncultivated herbs where they are found

Winterizing: preparing plants for the winter season

Bibliography

Chevallier, Andrew. *Encyclopedia of Herbal Medicine.*
New York: DK Publishing Inc. 2000.

Gardening by the Moon. **www.gardeningbythemoon.com**.
Accessed August 1, 2010.

Gladstar, Rosemary. *Herbal Recipes for Vibrant Health.*
North Adams, Massachusetts: Storey Publishing. 2008.

Green, James. *The Herbal Medicine-Maker's Handbook.*
Freedom, California: Crossing Press. 2000.

Hartung, Tammi. *Growing 101 Herbs that Heal.*
North Adams, Massachusetts: Storey Publishing. 2000.

National Geographic. **www.nationalgeographic.com**.
Accessed August 1, 2010.

Smith, Miranda. *Your Backyard Herb Garden.*
Emmaus, Pennsylvania: Rodale Press, Inc. 1997.

Wendy M. Vincent is a freelance writer with a background in corporate communications, public relations, event planning and project management. She holds a bachelor's degree in communications with a minor in international languages and cultures as well as master's degree in liberal studies. In addition to being a regular contributor to *Renaissance Magazine*, she also writes for several online travel-related publications from her home in the Connecticut woods. Her other titles include an upcoming travel guide to Mystic, Conn. (Channel Lake, 2011).

Descended from generations of home gardeners and farmers, Vincent has a yard abundant in perennial and vegetable gardens. Additionally, she has created a dedicated herb garden to use for cultivating healing and medicinal herbs for personal and family use. She uses her homegrown herbs in everyday cooking and to treat common ailments. Vincent has an extensive book collection on herbs and has attended numerous workshops, classes and festivals dedicated to growing and using herbs.

Index